Praise for

Evan Carmichael

"Evan consumes so much content and then knows how to DJ it to inspire people."

—GARY VAYNERCHUK

"Evan, you have a lot of entrepreneurs in your audience. They're listening to figure out how to add more value."

—TONY ROBBINS

"Napoleon Hill was the single greatest influence of all time in personal development. Evan is the modern day Napoleon Hill."

—ED MYLETT

"If you're listening to Evan that means you're into success. If you're a friend of Evan's, you're a friend of mine!"

—GRANT CARDONE

BUILT
TO
SERVE

FIND YOUR PURPOSE
AND BECOME THE LEADER
YOU WERE BORN TO BE

EVAN CARMICHAEL

#BELIEVE

A SAVIO REPUBLIC BOOK
An Imprint of Post Hill Press

Built to Serve:
Find Your Purpose and Become the Leader You Were Born to Be
© 2020 by Evan Carmichael
All Rights Reserved

ISBN: 978-1-64293-491-5
ISBN (eBook): 978-1-64293-492-2

Interior graphics by Jason 'J-Ryze' Fonceca
Cover photography by Honeysuckle Photography, Maggie Kirkland
Interior design and composition, Greg Johnson, Textbook Perfect

posthillpress.com
New York • Nashville

Published in the United States of America

DO YOU WANT FREE BONUSES?

*"Find a way to get paid for doing what you love.
Then every paycheck will be a bonus."*

—OPRAH WINFREY

Thank you for buying my latest book!

You're about to go on an amazing journey of self-discovery, and to celebrate you as well as thank you, I'm giving away a number of *free bonuses* with this book, including:

- PDF worksheets for every exercise in this book that you can print out and follow along as you read.
- A private Facebook group where you can meet like-minded people and where I'll be posting content and hosting live Q&A sessions.
- Bonus videos of coaching sessions helping people find their *Who*, *Why*, *How*, and helping them build their business.
- Entry for prizes to win one-on-one time with me, autographed books, and other goodies!

To get the bonuses just send an email with your book receipt or a picture with you holding the book to serve@evancarmichael.com, and we'll set you up.

Thank you once again for your support, and strap in for an incredible journey!

Much love,

Evan

#Believe

WHAT IS MY PURPOSE?

"Efforts and courage are not enough
without purpose and direction."

—JOHN F. KENNEDY

What is my purpose? How do I find my passion?

Hundreds of millions of people have viewed my videos, read my books, and interacted with me at my events. By far, the number one question that people ask is some variation of, "What is my purpose?" or "How do I find my passion?"

You are not alone.

I've had people who were at rock bottom and homeless ask me this question. I've also met millionaires stuck on the same problem. Finding your purpose isn't something that discriminates. Everyone wants to find it. It's a human need.

Most people wake up and drive to a job they hate.

Think about your five closest friends. Are they happy? Do they live their lives with purpose? Do you? We put on a fake front for what we want people to see and think about us, but the reality is most people aren't happy. We're lost. We settle. You can't be happy if you don't know your purpose. It's not possible. You want more, but you don't even know where to start. You know there is more out there. You see others having success, and you want it too; there is nothing wrong with that. You just need help finding your purpose so you can find the success you see all around you. You can be productive, crush your goals, and pretend that all the things you've acquired actually mean something...but at the end of the day, if you don't know your purpose you'll always feel like there's something missing. You'll know that you're capable of more and that you're not living the life you should be. You might be fooling the world, but you're not fooling the person looking back at you in the mirror. You need to find your actual power source.

Your purpose is your source of power.

Once you find your purpose, it'll fuel you for life. You'll do things that you never thought you were capable of. Achieving your purpose will force you to morph into a stronger version of yourself. You'll have to push through the fears, insecurities, and doubts that have held you back. But somehow, it'll all feel possible and necessary because you're purpose driven now... and that's the only thing you'll ever need.

Take it from me. I'm a scared introvert who wants to reach the world.

I'M A SCARED INTROVERT

"My worst trait is that I'm an introvert. When I've led stuff, the hardest thing for me to overcome has been my natural desire to run and hide."

—SHONDA RHIMES

I hate the spotlight.

I'm introverted and hate the attention being on me. I'm not the life of the party. I don't talk to the person next to me on an airplane. I never go to networking meetings. I can't stand small talk.

But I'm also on a mission.

I'm trying to solve the world's biggest problem: I want people to #Believe in themselves. I want to reach a billion people. The biggest complaint I used to get from my agent was, "Evan, the problem with you is you don't want to be famous. You don't crave the attention." He was right. I have no desire to be famous. I don't want attention. But after years of listening to him pounding on me, I finally heard his message. What he was really saying was, *Evan, if you want to spread your mission, you need to get famous. If you blow up, so does your message.* It finally connected for me. He was right. But I was afraid.

I'm afraid of disappointing people.

My biggest fear is that I'll let people down. The thought that someone would spend money on something I made (like this book!) and not get amazing value from it destroys me. The plus side is that I always do my best to over-deliver and give people way more value than they paid for. The downside is I'm afraid to act because each time I do there's a possibility that I'll let someone down.

So how does an introvert who is afraid of disappointing people get famous?

To be honest, I don't have all the answers. But I'm attacking those fears head on. Because my purpose demands that I do. It took me 350 videos on my YouTube channel before I wasn't completely embarrassed by myself. I forced myself to learn from people who I disagreed with because they still had something important to teach me. I did a ninety-day speaking tour across twenty-three cities to take on my fear of letting people down. Every four days, I went to a new city and risked failure when I took the stage. I finished the last month of my tour even though I had broken my neck in two spots, compressed my spine, suffered a concussion, and had three staples in my head. I'm not superhuman. I'm a scared introvert. But my purpose forced me into action mode and gave me the strength to take on my biggest fears. Your purpose will do the same for you.

Understand that the world has changed, and now it's actually possible.

THE WORLD HAS CHANGED

"The sooner we realize that the world has changed, the sooner we can accept it and make something of what we've got. Whining isn't a scalable solution."

—SETH GODIN

Young people don't want to end up like their parents.

They don't want to stick with one company forever. It doesn't make sense to them. And the people in my middle-aged audience also don't want to end up like their parents. They want to escape the confines of the job they took out of college. We all are feeling held back, stuck in complacency.

For generations, we have turned to our parents and grandparents for advice.

We could depend on them to know the answers and steer us in the right direction. But in the past two decades, the world has transformed completely. The rules people lived by no longer apply. The opportunities open to you were not available when your parents were your age. Staying in the job you got out of college until you retire doesn't make sense anymore. Technology has changed how we live, buy, work, and even raise families.

Generations of people are looking for answers—the very answers that are in this book.

Humans are built to serve.

Some people are built to serve the world. Others want to serve the twenty-five closest people to them. But in either case, humans are built to serve. If you're not happy right now, it's because you're not serving enough people, or you're not serving the people in your life deeply enough. But whom do you serve? How do you serve? And once you've found the answers to these questions, how can you make money serving so you can help even more people? That's what we're going to figure out together in this book.

The process you're about to go through is eye opening and replicable.

Anyone, at any stage in their life, can apply it to their own lives. You are currently three steps away from true fulfillment. I've been helping people for twenty years in my work with entrepreneurs, and that work has built this process from the ground up. It's a method that has helped my content reach hundreds of millions of people around the world and led to institutions like *Forbes* and *Inc.* magazine calling me one of the best speakers on the planet. It's a simple, repeatable, foolproof method that helps people who come in feeling lost leave feeling transformed. I know that these three steps work. They worked for me, and I've seen them help thousands of people. Now, they can work for you too.

I will show you step by step how to find purpose using the **Who, Why, How** *process.*

WHO, WHY, HOW

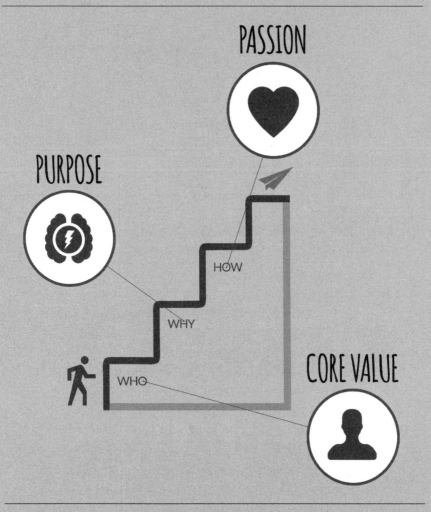

PASSION

PURPOSE

HOW

WHY

CORE VALUE

WHO

YOUR JOURNEY BEGINS

STEP 1: YOUR *WHO*

"Today you are you! That is truer than true! There is no
one alive who is you-er than you!"

—DR. SEUSS

Everybody has Michael Jordan-level talent...
at something.

You just haven't found it yet, or you have and you don't #Believe
in yourself enough to go all in on it. You're a genius. You're
amazing. You were not meant to live a photocopy of someone
else's life. You were not created to wake up and do work that is
below your capabilities. You have Michael Jordan-level talent at
something and need to uncover exactly what your purpose is
and how you can serve.

I'll start this process by asking you what your most
important core value is.

What do you stand for? What is your single most important core
value? Most people have no idea. They've never been asked that
question before. So I'll ask probing questions like, "Who was
your favorite teacher growing up? What is your favorite movie
of all time? What is your favorite song?"

Everything great that you love is connected.

For example, you don't love Mrs. Jones because she taught you eighth-grade math. You love her because she was the only teacher who didn't make you feel like an outsider. She made you feel like you *belonged*. Now it makes sense why your favorite movie is *Hercules*, because he was half-god, half-human and never felt like he *belonged* in either the land of the gods or the humans. Now it makes sense why "Go the Distance" by Michael Bolton is your favorite song, because that line, "When I go the distance, I'll be right where I belong," always hits you emotionally. Your most important core value is *belonging*.

This is powerful.

When I do this live with people, at this point they're usually stunned. How did this stranger break them down so quickly in five minutes, when they've lived their entire life without knowing what they stand for? How does so much of their life now suddenly make sense, when they felt lost only moments before?

Finding your most important core value is what I call your *Who*.

It's finding who you are. And knowing that you stand for *belonging* allows you to set a course for your life. You now know that being in a business, a job, a relationship where you don't feel like you belong is going to be toxic for you, no matter how much money you make or how much you look like you're winning by any other metric. It's a life-changing experience for people.

But we're just getting started. Now we need to find your **Why.**

STEP 2: YOUR *WHY*

"There are two great days in a person's life—the day
we are born and the day we discover why."

— WILLIAM BARCLAY

Next, I'll ask you what the most painful moment of your life was.

When I do this in my workshops, it requires courage from people. They're standing up in a room full of strangers, being asked to share their most intimate, private, painful moment of all time. They're afraid to share it, but for some reason they want to, because in those five minutes we've built up enough rapport where they feel safe. Some people know exactly what their most painful moment was. Others have no idea. They've never been asked this question before and they've buried the pain so deep that they don't want to live it again. But eventually it comes out. For example, you moved to America from overseas as a young child and were bullied for your accent and for being different. You felt like an outsider and that you never *belonged*. There's that word again! I explain that your purpose comes from your pain—that your greatest joy in life will come from helping others who currently are going through the pain that you went through. In this example, your purpose is to help outsiders feel like they belong.

People often need a moment at this point.

Many people start crying. It's like I just looked into their soul and touched them at the core of who they are. Their entire life, they had no idea what they should do, and they suffered in silence. In ten minutes together, we just figured everything out. They realize that they have worth, that their struggle could actually be helpful, and that maybe, for the first time in their life, they could feel empowered and important. This is what I call your *Why*. Your purpose comes from your pain, and we'll find it together in this book.

Your *Who* and your *Why* don't change.

They're with you for life. When you're ninety-five years old, you won't stop caring about *belonging*. In fact, it'll likely only become stronger as you gain more confidence with it. You also won't stop wanting to help outsiders feel like they belong. You'll only double down on it as you gain more wisdom and strength with time. Your *Who* and your *Why* tell you who you are and your purpose for the rest of your life. They are incredibly powerful, and they give you more self-awareness than 99 percent of the world has right now.

But we're still not done. Now we need to find your How.

STEP 3: YOUR *HOW*

"It does not matter how slowly you go
as long as you do not stop."

—CONFUCIUS

The final step is finding out how you got through the pain you suffered.

You were an outsider with an accent who didn't fit in and were bullied. How did you get through it? How did you cope? You're so much stronger now than you were. You have a thicker skin, more self-confidence, massive resilience. How? What did you do? You might say that it was hard. That you weren't always like this. But through meditation you fixed it. Amazing! This is the start of what I call your *How*. How you got through that terrible situation is teachable. You can show others how to do it as well. Maybe you sell meditation videos, create a meditation center, teach at a meditation school, host meditation retreats, or any number of options. But the exact meditation that pulled you out is a recipe to pull others out too. And as you continue to find new ways to make outsiders feel like they belong, you can teach, sell, and help more people. Your *How* is your passion. It's what you will love to do everyday to help others. Your *How* will evolve. In 2020, maybe it's selling meditation retreats. In 2030, maybe it's virtual reality and holographic versions of you beaming into people's living rooms. Your *Who* and *Why* are constant. Your *How* will evolve as technology, markets, and you evolve.

Lee from Atlanta was a college dropout who didn't know what to do next in his life. He had a job as a car salesman but wasn't fulfilled. We discovered that his *Who* (core value) was trust. His *Why* (most painful moment) was being held back in school and always feeling like he had something to prove. His *How* (passion) was studying success, which inspired him to become an achiever. He became the car salesman who sells to achievers who have something to prove and wins by building immediate trust with them.

Ronni from Salt Lake City realized that her *Who* was joy. Her *Why* was that she was abused as a child and fell victim to abuse again in her first marriage. As a child, she would decorate her room like a fantasyland that she could escape to. She went on to study interior design, and I helped her find her *How*—a new business as the interior designer for children who are victims of abuse and are now healing. She could create fantasylands for them to find joy, just like she did for herself growing up.

John from Tulsa was successful but not fulfilled. It looked like he had it all: a huge house, millions of dollars, a great family. But he couldn't connect his work to a purpose. I found that his *Who* was peace. His *Why* was being an immigrant from a war-torn country who had to leave his family behind. His *How* has been to connect people on both sides of the war to make peace happen. Now he wants to spread a message of peace around the world. He has just started as a speaker and is taking stages to start to share his story. For the first time he feels like a real success.

Are you ready to step onto the big stage, Michael Jordan? Let's find out who you are!

STEP 1

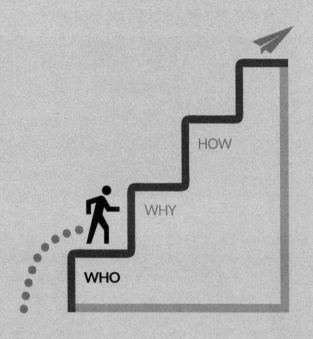

YOUR WHO

YOUR WHO = YOUR CORE VALUE

"Better than a thousand hollow words,
is one word that brings peace."

—BUDDHA

You have one core value that defines who you are. I call it your *Who*.

People are defined by their values. But you have one core value that is more important than all others. It's the starting point for all your ideas, actions, and beliefs. If you're ever in a slump, it's because you're living your life inconsistently with your *Who*, your most important core value.

This is the starting point for everything.

If you're confused about what to do next; if you're pressured by others to fit in or live their version of your life; if you feel held back because of people judging you, it's because you don't know who you are or what you stand for.

Your *Who* is your rock.

Most people live on quicksand. They're constantly moving, but the more they move and struggle, the more they feel like they're sinking. When you figure out your *Who*, you have a solid rock to stand on. Suddenly you have clarity about your direction. You stop being pulled into other people's agendas because you have your own map now. You don't allow the opinions of others to damage your self-worth because you stand for something now. You know what the right thing to do is because your *Who* demands it. Having clarity over who you are is your source of power.

So how do you find your *Who*?

I've written an entire book on this topic called *Your One Word.* It's definitely worth a read and goes in depth on not just how to find your *Who*, but how to apply it to your life and business. It also shows how five businesses with revenues from $50,000 to hundreds of millions of dollars use their *Who* to build meaningful businesses that make money and have a positive impact. I'm going to summarize the process of finding your *Who* here in two powerful exercises, but if you want to dive deeper, my first book will help.

Let's start by figuring out what makes you happy.

WHAT MAKES YOU HAPPY?

"The Constitution only gives people the right to pursue happiness. You have to catch it yourself."

—BENJAMIN FRANKLIN

This page is very important. This exercise is life-changing.

Let's start by having you answer five essential questions. You need to actually write these answers down, so pull out the worksheets (go to the start of this book for instructions on how to get your free worksheets) or go get a piece of paper. Put the book down and go get it. It's worth it. I promise. Then answer these questions:

1. Who was your favorite teacher growing up and why?
2. What is your favorite movie of all time?
3. What do you love most about how your parents raised you?
4. Which successful person do you look up to as a role model and why?
5. For your kids (current or future), what lessons do you want to make sure they understand?

What does this have to do with figuring out your *Who*?

Everything. All the great things in your life are connected. Your job is to find what that connection is. What does your favorite teacher have to do with your favorite movie? What does your role model have to do with the lessons you want to teach your kids? *Everything.* In looking at your answers to the five questions, what stands out? What single most important core value do they all have in common?

If you can't find it yet, try this.

Next to each of the answers list three description words—just single words, not sentences. Three words on why that person is your favorite teacher. Three words on why you love that movie. Three words for what you love about how your parents raised you...and so on. Five questions. Three words each. You should have fifteen words in front of you now. If not, go do it. This is important.

Then, underline the repeated words.

Look at your list of fifteen words and underline the ones that come up more than once. This is the start of the connection. Anything that comes up repeatedly gives you clarity on what your *Who* is. If you have multiple words that are underlined, does one have more meaning to you than the other? Could one be the parent of the other, or are they both equal in your mind? If they're both equal, then what word could be the parent to both of them? Get it down to one word. Clarity is power.

Here's an example from Aleks, an entrepreneur I invested in who runs Toronto Dance Salsa, one of the largest salsa-dancing schools in the world.

THE 5 ESSENTIAL QUESTIONS

1
WHO WAS YOUR **FAVORITE TEACHER** GROWING UP, & WHY?

2
WHAT IS YOUR **FAVORITE MOVIE** OF ALL TIME?

3
WHAT DO YOU LOVE MOST ABOUT HOW YOUR **PARENTS RAISED YOU?**

4
WHICH SUCCESSFUL PERSON DO YOU **LOOK UP TO,** & WHY?

5
WHAT LESSONS DO YOU WANT **YOUR KIDS** TO HAVE?
(CURRENT, FUTURE, OR BORROWED)

WHAT MAKES ALEKS HAPPY?

"Belonging is about self-acceptance...not fitting in."

—ALEKS SAIYAN

Who was your favorite teacher growing up and why?

My favorite teacher was John Fischer. He believed in me. Outside of our regular science classes, he supported me. He helped me create the first Go Club (kind of like Chinese chess), where I made friends. He made me feel included and was like a father to me by giving advice and a friendly ear when I needed it. *Three words: Belief, Open Arms, Belong.*

What is your favorite movie of all time?

My favorite movie is Disney's *Hercules* (1997). Three words: *Belong, Hero, Self-acceptance.*

What do you love most about how your parents raised you?

My mom taught me to reflect on my actions and that there is more than one way to see a conflict. I'm not always right. Three words: *Understanding, Care, Patience.*

Which successful person do you look up to as a role model and why?

Kevin Hart. He hustles hard at everything he does but has fun in the process. I want to be just like that—have an endless hunger with endless fun. Three words: *Self-acceptance, Hero, Belong*.

For your kids (current or future), what lessons do you want to make sure they understand?

- Pick friends who make you feel stronger and lift you up.
- Belonging is about self-acceptance...not fitting in.
- Be open and tell others when you feel scared or unsure.
- When someone doesn't like you, most of the time it's not you, they just don't like something about themselves.
- When you're afraid, it means it's important; you will survive.
- Do things that scare you and make you uncomfortable.
- Three words: *Understanding, Self-acceptance, Belong*.

Most repeated words: Belong (four), Self-acceptance (three), Understanding (two), Hero (two). Aleks ended up going with #Belong and is building his entire life and business around it.

Happy doesn't always lead to your Who, though, so you may find it easier to go negative instead.

WHAT DO YOU HATE?

"We must concentrate not merely on the negative
expulsion of war but the positive affirmation of peace."

—MARTIN LUTHER KING JR.

If you can't find your *Who* by going positive, think about what you hate.

Make a list of all the people you can't stand being around—an old boss, a bully in school, a bad teacher, a family member, a roommate, and other people who feel or act a certain way. You don't need to be angry with them or think they're bad people. There's just something about them that you don't want to be around. It's toxic to you.

What's the most toxic thing these people have in common?

Do they lie? Are they fake? Do they insult people? Do they cheat? Do they steal? Do they complain? Do they have no ambition? Are they self-defeating? Are they unethical? Do they put others down? What is it?

Draw the line that connects the people you can't stand being around.

Do the same exercise of making a list of five people, writing three descriptive words for each of them, then looking at your list of fifteen words and underlining the common ones. Whatever comes up the most is your *Anti-Word*. The opposite is your core value, your *Who*.

I've never seen someone's *Who* be something negative.

Humans are built to serve. We're good at the core. We want to do good and so do our neighbors. We're just confused about how to do it and are stressed out living lives that don't have meaning. If your *Anti-Word* is "lie," maybe your *Who* is "honesty" or "truth." "Fake" becomes "genuine." "Insulting" becomes "supportive." And so on.

Find Your *Who*.

It's the core of who you are. Your decisions looking back now will make a lot more sense and you'll have more clarity and direction moving forward instead of living an accidental life. If it doesn't come right away or you're not sure, sleep on it. With every night that goes by, it should feel more and more right. If it doesn't, you picked the wrong *Who*, and you need to review the exercise again.

Now, let me tell you about my Who: #Believe.

#BELIEVE

"Whether you believe you can do a thing or not,
you are right."

—HENRY FORD

Here are my answers to the five essential questions:

1. My favorite teacher was Madame Farr. She always made time for me, connected with me one on one, and helped me navigate the difficulties of high school.

2. My favorite movie is *Seabiscuit*. It's about a horse that was too small, a jockey that was too big, and an owner and trainer who were down on their luck. They somehow all find each other and end up winning against all odds, lifting a nation. I've seen the movie at least thirty times.

3. What I love most about how my parents raised me was, whenever I was doing poorly in school or was sad or disappointed, they would tell me that I was *Evan Castrilli Carmichael*, and I could do anything that I put my mind to.

4. My favorite entrepreneur of all time is A.P. Giannini. He was the founder of Bank of America. He lent money to hard-working immigrants when no bank would. He bet on people based on a look in their eye and a handshake. He gave Walt

Disney the money to launch the first feature-length cartoon when everyone thought he was nuts. I called Bank of America's PR department to do a story on him for my YouTube channel and they had no idea who he was.

5. Whenever I put my son Hayden to sleep or drop him off somewhere, I have a ritual where I'll say, "Carmichaels can do..." and he'll finish the sentence with, "Anything!"

Notice a common thread through my answers?

Does #Believe pop out clearly in each story? That's my core value. That's my *Who*. It's who I've always been and always will be. When I discovered it, I was able to create a better plan for myself with more intention. Whether I say the word or not, #Believe is a part of everything I make. My content is about #Believe. My workshops are about #Believe. My team is about #Believe. This book is about #Believe. Everything I touch always has a positive, optimistic, hopeful, encouraging vibe to it. Because that's who I am.

But what happens when making money goes against your Who?

YOUR *WHO* > MONEY

"Make money your god,
and it will plague you like the devil."

—HENRY FIELDING

There has to be something that's more important to you than money.

I don't think people grow up with a healthy perspective on money. Some people grow up thinking money is everything and you need to do whatever it takes to get yours. Others will say that money is the root of all...evil. Did you complete the sentence in your head before reading it?

Money is just a tool. And it's a very important one.

Money is important. Even if you're a charity, money is important. It's just not number one. But it's also not number one hundred. Money should be in your top five priorities. If you're an entrepreneur and it's not, you'll never build a successful business. But it's not number one. Something has to come before it. That's your *Who*. That's your most important core value.

Let's use me as an example.

The content I make is always positive. It's educational. It's #Believe. But most people would rather escape from their challenges by entertaining themselves instead of fixing their problems by educating themselves. If I made a "Top 10 Stupidest Things _____ Said" video, I could get more views than a "Top 10 Rules for Success" on the same person. It would bring me more money in the short term. And I'd feel gross doing it. I haven't done it because I have clarity on my *Who*. I'm about #Believe.

That's what makes me come alive. That's what I stand for.

When difficult situations arise, your *Who* becomes the filter through which you make the difficult decisions. It makes every decision easier, and it gives you the confidence to move forward, because you're standing on your rock and other people can't move you from it no matter how much money or temptation they throw at you. So I'm about #Believe. And every person, including you, has their own individual *Who*, no matter how rich or poor, famous or unknown you are.

Let's take a look at the Who that brings Tony Robbins happiness: #Progress.

#PROGRESS

"I always tell people if you want to know the secret
to happiness, I can give it to you in one word:
Progress. Progress equals happiness."

—TONY ROBBINS

Tony Robbins knows a thing or two about #Progress.

His parents divorced when he was seven years old. Money was always tight. His mother was an alcoholic and very abusive. He had a number of different step-fathers. At seventeen, he ran away from home because his mom chased him out of the house with a knife. He had to support himself, so he went to work as a janitor. He then discovered the motivational speaker Jim Rohn, who became his first mentor. He studied under Jim, applied his methods, started helping others, and set down his path to make a positive contribution to the world by giving people progress. Today, top CEOs pay him over a million dollars per year to coach them, he spends over 200 days a year traveling around the world selling out arenas for his events, and he has multiple bestselling books on everything from personal development to managing money. Tony's story is one of massive #Progress, and now he helps others make #Progress in their lives as well.

So how does Tony deal with achieving goals? Through #Progress. Robbins tells CNBC:

"There are levels of making it in life and whatever you think 'making it' is, when you get there, you'll see there's another level. That never ends, because if you stop growing, you're going to be unhappy. When you achieve a goal, it feels good for—how long? You know, a week? A month? Six months? A year? And then it doesn't feel so good. I don't care what it is you've achieved, and the reason is because life is not about achieving the goals, life is about who you become in pursuit of those goals."

How does he deal with his up and coming competitors? Same thing. #Progress.

"I have a lot of young bucks that come up to me sometimes—you know, in their 20s or 30s—[and] they go: 'You remember me! I'm going to get to where you are!' And I say, 'Well, I think that's wonderful. I hope you do. When you get to where I am, you'll be where I was because I'm not going to stop growing. So let's grow together!' That's really my approach."

When you see every problem through the lens of your *Who*, the solution becomes so much more obvious.

It works for me. It works for Tony Robbins. It can work for you too.

There's one more critical step to your finding your Who, though, and that's your Credo.

YOUR CREDO

"Nonviolence is the first article of my faith.
It is also the last article of my creed."

—MAHATMA GANDHI

Want to know the biggest regret I have from my first book, *Your One Word*?

It was not giving your *Credo* a more prominent role, because it's extremely important. So what is your *Credo*? It's how you break down your *Who*. You start with your core value, then you add some definition to it by adding the three things that make it up.

Did you notice that I always put a "#" before my *Who* of #Believe?

It's because "believe" means something to most people, but "#Believe" means something more to me. I get to define the difference between "believe" and "#Believe." I call it the *Credo*. I break down my *Who* of #Believe into my three-part *Credo* of believing in yourself (self-confidence), believing in your work (passion), and believing that it's going to work out (conviction). Most people would just think about "believe" as "believe in yourself (self-confidence)." And it's that for me, but it's also so much more. Whichever *Who* you pick, there will always be a general understanding of what that word means, but to you it will always mean so much more. Creating your *Credo* gives you more clarity for your decisions as well as the message you spread to attract the right people to you.

Your Turn: What's Your *Credo*?

To finish up your *Who*, you need to finalize your own *Credo*. Think about what your core value is, and then come up with three definitions of it. Three examples of it. Three children of it. #Believe equals self-confidence, passion, and conviction to me. What does your *Who* mean to you? (And as a quick side note, if you haven't found your *Who* yet and are stuck on two or three that are all equal for you, consider that those words could make up your *Credo* and there's a more powerful, all-encompassing *Who* that sits above them.)

How to use your *Credo*.

Your *Credo* gives you extra clarity. Now when you're making important decisions, you have a deeper understanding of what your *Who* actually is. When you're spreading your message through your marketing or hiring process, you can better articulate what you are all about so you can start getting the right people to you who believe the same things you do. Everything you do should go through one of the three paths of your *Credo* if you want to feel fulfilled from your actions. And if you're unhappy, it's because you're not doing the work that passes through the three parts of your *Credo*. It's that simple and that powerful.

Let's now apply this to your life so it makes more sense.

YOUR CREDO: 3 KEY PILLARS

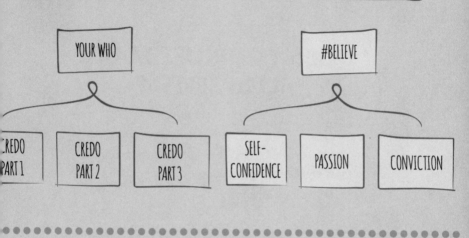

YOUR WHO

#BELIEVE

CREDO PART 1 | CREDO PART 2 | CREDO PART 3

SELF-CONFIDENCE | PASSION | CONVICTION

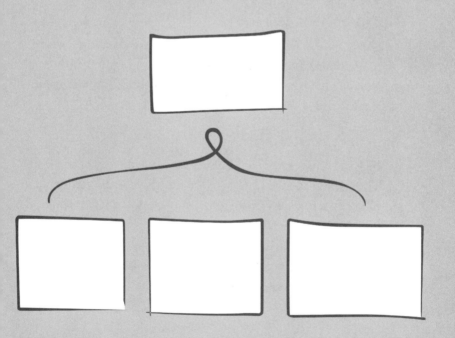

DOES YOUR LIFE MAKE MORE SENSE?

"If there's something that I want to do, but somehow can't get myself to do, it's because I don't have clarity."

—GRETCHEN RUBIN

This is where it gets scary.

You have your *Who*. You have your *Credo* to break down what your *Who* means to you. Now let's run your life through those filters. You know the life you want to be leading, but how are you measuring up?

Start with your career.

What kind of work are you doing? Are you an employee? Do you have your own business? How are the clients you work with? What about your colleagues? How are the projects you're working on? Where is most of your working time spent? Are you happy at work? If you're not happy, the answer is your *Who*. If your *Who* is #Freedom, you're not going to do well in a workplace that has lots of structure and rules. If your *Who* is #Honesty, you'll be unhappy with people around you who lie and play office politics. Your *Who* is the key to understanding the source of your unhappiness.

Then go to your friendships.

Who are you hanging with outside of work? Are they the same people that you knew from kindergarten? If your *Who* is #Loyalty, you're probably happy. If your *Who* is #Growth, and your friends haven't grown like you have, you're probably unhappy and are in these friendships out of convenience. You need to move on. Your growth, purpose, and happiness depend on it. Hopefully examples like these show you how important it is to run your life through your *Credo*. It makes everything clearer.

Next up are your parents and close family.

A piece of your *Who* is rooted in your childhood. Either you want to emulate a characteristic that you loved about your parents, or you want to be the exact opposite of them. If you're unhappy with your relationship with your parents, start by trying to understand their *Who*. Know that they probably love you. They're just running their advice through their *Who* filter. If their *Who* is #Stability because they had none growing up and your *Who* is #Creativity, you're going to clash. You may see it as them being negative and holding back your dreams, but they love you. Meet them with compassion where they're at. It doesn't mean you have to agree with them, but understanding their *Who* takes the sting out of their words. They're actually trying to support you. They just are running on a different operating system.

And how about the most important person in your life?

WHO DID YOU MARRY?

"Marry the right person. This one decision will deter-
mine 90% of your happiness or misery."

—H. JACKSON BROWN JR.

Who you marry is the family you choose.

You didn't pick your parents. You didn't choose your siblings,
cousins, aunts, and uncles. Most of us still feel an obligation
to spend time with our birth family, even if we have totally
different *Whos*. In most cultures, you pick the person you marry.
Your spouse is the family you choose, and it's one of the most
important decisions you'll ever make.

So many successful people credit their spouse for being essential to their success.

"Obviously I couldn't have done anything that I've done without
Michelle. What keeps me sane, what keeps me balanced, what
allows me to deal with the pressure. It is this young lady right
here…Not only has she been a great first lady, she is just my
rock. I count on her in so many ways every single day."

—*Barack Obama, on his wife Michelle*

"Priscilla's the most important person in my life, so you can say it's the most important thing I built in my time here."

—*Mark Zuckerberg, on his wife Priscilla*

"I would not be the woman I am if I did not go home to that man. It just gives me such a foundation."

—*Beyoncé, on her husband Jay-Z*

It's also backed up by science.

According to a study by Carnegie Mellon University, people with supportive spouses are "more likely to give themselves the chance to succeed." They studied 163 married couples and found that people with supportive spouses were more likely to take on potentially rewarding challenges. Those who accepted challenges experienced more personal growth, happiness, and psychological well-being.

But most people don't know how to choose properly.

Over 40 percent of marriages end in divorce. Many more marriages continue on out of convenience rather than love and support. What keeps couples together? Shared values. You don't need to have the exact same *Who*, but they need to be related. Otherwise there's not enough common ground. Looks fade. Hobbies change. Your *Who* stays constant. What you do might change many times, but the way you approach it will stay constant because of your *Who*. Your *Who* is the path to finding your ideal partner.

Knowing this, are you ready to make some tough decisions?

THIS WILL BE TOUGH

"You have to have confidence, and then be tough
enough to follow through."

—ROSALYNN CARTER

We just put a giant magnifying glass on your life.

If you did the exercises, then you know your *Who*. You know
how it breaks down. You know where your career and life don't
match up, and you know the source of your unhappiness.

Now what?

Now comes change. And that's tough. Do you have the courage
to do what's needed? Are you willing to start that business?
Fire that client? Buy out your business partner? Let go of some
friends? Seek to understand your parents? Get divorced? It may
not be that serious for you, but...

The greater your unhappiness, the greater your actions will need to be.

You're not living the life that you want. You need to be coura-
geous enough to make the change. Knowing alone is not enough.
Action is required.

Your *Who* will give you the courage.

Here's what's going to happen: You'll find multiple areas that you know you need to change. You now know why you need to change them and the source of your unhappiness. But when it comes time to actually act, chances are you won't.

Have you ever heard the phrase, "The chains of habit are too light to be felt until they are too heavy to be broken"? It's true for most people. Because you'll tell yourself that this life isn't so bad, right? It's not exactly what you want, but who gets exactly what they want? What if you can't do the thing you want? What if you can't attract the people you want into your life? You need to end this thinking. It's keeping you small and preventing you from pursuing your purpose. Your *Who* gives you courage. When you doubt yourself, look at your *Who*. Look at your *Credo*. Remind yourself of who you are and that it's time to take the chains off. You've been running your entire life with your hands tied behind your back and it's time to explode forward. You're ready. You've been ready for some time now. You're just not used to it and it's scary. That's ok. Go back to your *Who*. It's your energy source. Never forget who you are. It's who you've always been and always will be.

Your Who is also what you would tell your younger self if you had the chance.

WHAT WOULD YOU TELL YOUNGER YOU?

"Evan, if you could travel back in time to talk to your
younger self, what message would you bring?"

—ONE OF THE MOST FREQUENT QUESTIONS
I GET ASKED IN INTERVIEWS

I used to hate this question.

First of all, I don't think this way. I don't think backwards. I
can't go back and talk to my younger self, so who cares? I spend
zero time looking in the rear-view mirror and use all my energy
driving forward, keeping my eyes on the road. I'm also so grateful
for my life right now that I wouldn't change anything. If I went
back in time, maybe it would break the space-time continuum
and when I came back, maybe I'd be a janitor working for the
robots who rule the world, and I'd hate my life. Who knows?

There is only one answer to the question.

It's your *Who*. My *Who* is #Believe. So if I had to go back, my
message to myself would be #Believe. #Believe in yourself more.
#Believe in your ideas more. #Believe in your abilities more.

Have the courage to follow your *Who*. Self-awareness and the boldness to follow through are the greatest gifts you can give yourself. That's the best possible answer to a useless question.

Then I found out how to love this question.

Here's where it flipped for me. After answering this same question for the thousandth time in an interview, I took it one step further. I asked myself, *What if eighty-five-year-old Evan from the future could come back and talk to present-day Evan? What would his message to me be?* And the answer blew me away. It's still my *Who*. It's still #Believe. Eighty-five-year-old Evan would tell present day Evan to #Believe in yourself more. #Believe in your ideas more. #Believe in your abilities more. It's a reminder to have more courage today. Right now. To say yes. To do the things I'm afraid to do. I want to meet eighty-five-year-old Evan and be proud of what I became. I want to know that I hit my potential instead of wasting it by being afraid.

It's the same thing for you.

Your advice should be your *Who*. Looking backwards is just a brain exercise, but thinking about the eighty-five-year-old version of you telling you the same message in the future should be inspiring. Your *Who* is who you are, but it's also aspirational. The more you take on, the more you're capable of taking on. What you thought was big and impossible becomes nothing a year later as you're growing and taking on new challenges. Your *Who* is a constant, never-ending drive to expand what you're capable of.

Here's part of a letter Oprah Winfrey wrote to her younger self.

DEAR BEAUTIFUL BROWN-SKINNED GIRL

For Oprah's entire letter to herself, please visit Oprah.com.
Oprah starts her letter to her younger self with...

> *"Dear beautiful brown-skinned girl. I look into your eyes
> and see the light and hope of myself."*

She tells herself that she's almost twenty and reflects on her just
being hired as a reporter for a TV station. She's scared that she'll
be unable to handle her classwork and career, but most of all
she's worried about her relationship.

> *"He seems less than impressed."*

She's worried, she's doubting herself, and it's not the first or last
time that she'll play small based off of someone else's opinion
of her. She's frustrated that she doesn't love herself and instead
finds love by doing what other people want her to do. She wrote,

> *"A lesson you will have to learn again and again: to see
> yourself with your own eyes, to love yourself from your
> own heart."*

It came from her past. She was raped, molested, and whipped for
not doing as she was told and she wasn't allowed to show any

emotions to her family. As a result, she has no self-esteem and tries to please others to find worthiness. But she ends with love and encouragement for herself. She wrote,

> *"From where I sit now, viewing your journey, there are few regrets. Only months before this picture was taken, you wrote a poem about a 'woman becoming.' Even then you understood that success was a process and that moving with the flow of life and not against it would be your greatest achievement. Love you deeply, Oprah."*

I love the beautiful ending to the letter. For Oprah, it shows heart. It shows compassion. It shows hope. The close of a letter to yourself is the most powerful because it's usually what you need the most.

Let me give you my take on Oprah's letter to herself.

MY TAKE ON OPRAH'S LETTER

"Everything in the letter is still applicable
to Oprah today."

—EVAN CARMICHAEL

Everything Oprah wrote still applies to her life now.

At the core of her message is loving herself from her own heart. So let's say Oprah's *Who* is #Heart. Let's define her *Credo* as:

- You have a higher calling that will sustain and fill you. (Purpose)
- You are a woman becoming. (Change)
- You must move with the flow of life. (Action)
- #Heart = Purpose, Change, and Action.

That outline would have given her twenty-year-old self more confidence.

How should she handle this new job as a reporter? How should she deal with her boyfriend who is intimidated by her success? How should she stop seeing herself through his eyes and love herself? Through #Heart. Through purpose, change, and action.

Go back to when she was younger.

How should she handle years of her family wanting her to be something she's not? What should she do when she is raped? When she is told not to step out of place? When she is not allowed to show anger or cry? Same thing: #Heart. Love yourself through your eyes. Know you have a purpose. You must change. You need to act.

But this isn't just a letter looking backwards.

Everything in the letter is still applicable to Oprah today. Yes, she's not a brand new reporter anymore. Yes, she's not getting abused anymore. She certainly has allowed herself to cry and show her #Heart. But for as much success as Oprah Winfrey has had, she's not done. Not by a long shot. There is still a huge mountain ahead of her, and she's going to be unhappy if she doesn't climb it. Because she's about #Heart. Because she has a purpose and needs change and action. For someone like that, they're never done; they just continue to slay bigger dragons and continue to stretch their comfort zone. I love Oprah. She's done so much. And it's nothing compared to what she will do if she stays true to her *Who*. Your *Who* is aspirational but scary. It's a standard to live up to. It's a lifelong journey, and to stay on it you must constantly remind yourself of who you are.

You need a daily reminder of your Who and what it means to you.

OPRAH'S CREDO: #HEART

HEART

PURPOSE | CHANGE | ACTION

REMEMBER WHO
YOU ARE DAILY

"You are what you think all day long."

—RALPH WALDO EMERSON

It's too easy to forget your *Who.*

You might get inspired by reading this book, or by a conversation, or by watching a video, or by any number of things. But then you fall back to normal. If you're not consistent in your bold thinking, you won't be consistent in your bold actions. It's really hard to be in an environment of mediocrity and at the same time stay consistently inspired.

What's the fastest way to learn Italian?

Go to Italy. Sure, you can learn from books, classes, tutors, etc. But the fastest way is to just go to Italy. Surround yourself with it. Eliminate your options. Go find some small town where they don't speak English. You'll learn Italian in a hurry because you're forced to—because it's all around you, because you don't have any other options.

What's the fastest way to live your *Who*?

Same thing. No, I don't mean move to Italy. Create your own surroundings. What books do you read? What videos do you watch? Which events do you go to? What's your morning routine? Who do you hang out with? What's on your wall at home? How about at the office? What about in the car? What's on your cell phone or computer screens? These are all what I call *Play Bigger Triggers*. They're reminders in your environment of who you are, reminders to step up and play bigger!

Let's say your *Who* is #Care.

Watch a video every day of someone doing an act of kindness, then buy coffee for the person behind you in line. Every week, volunteer or help out at an event that has a cause you believe in. Put a sticker on your car steering wheel to #Care for your fellow drivers. Let them in when they signal. Never honk. Don't tailgate. Design your home and office by putting pictures up of people who inspire you to #Care more. Put a quote or graphic on your cell phone and computer. Surround yourself with things that remind you to #Care. When you're about to slip back into mediocrity, boom! There's a new reminder. It's everywhere. It's forcing you to become a better version of yourself. If every day you woke up and felt the strength and boldness of your *Who*, your life would look dramatically different one year from today. It will just happen. You won't be the same person in a year. You may not notice the shift on a day-to-day basis. You'll just feel happier, stronger, more confident. And over time, you'll see that the caterpillar became a butterfly.

I know because it happened to me.

HOW I #BELIEVE IN MYSELF

"The future belongs to those who believe
in the beauty of their dreams."

—ELEANOR ROOSEVELT

I created my YouTube channel for myself.

Every day, I post content profiling a different successful leader.
Why? Because I need it. I want to be around these people. My
Who is #Believe, and I want to be around it daily. I want to be
pulled up. When I'm watching a video of Elon Musk, Oprah
Winfrey, Steve Jobs, or any successful leader, it's a reminder to
#Believe in myself more. It's my daily *Play Bigger Trigger*.

**I ran a mastermind group in Toronto for over
a decade.**

It was designed for entrepreneurs who wanted advice and
support from other local entrepreneurs to help them grow. It was
a mix of advice and accountability. We met every month and
three of the people who joined the group in the first year were
still in the group a decade later.

In the last two years of the group, they told me that I changed.

My wife said the same thing. I was more direct. More bold. Pushing harder. Accepting fewer excuses. Playing bigger. I still #Believed in them and myself…just more. It wasn't an overnight shift, but an evolution of me becoming a more confident Evan.

How did I become that?

I watched the videos on my channel every day. I was getting pulled up by people who #Believed more than me. I injected myself with #Believe vitamin C daily so if mediocrity sneezed on me, I wouldn't get sick. I suffocated negativity and small thinking from my life. Whenever I thought I was thinking big, I'd see videos from people like Elon Musk talking about having a backup plan for the planet, and I realized I still had a long way to go. They were pushing me forward, forcing me to stretch and grow by association.

Proximity is power.

I haven't met Elon Musk or Oprah Winfrey. I haven't told Bill Gates that his story saved my first company. Not yet. But these people inspired me to #Believe harder in myself. And they still do. I'm nowhere near done. This is a lifelong adventure, and I wouldn't have it any other way. I'm excited to see where your adventures take you too!

*That's your **Who** and a demonstration of how powerful it is! Did you catch all of it? Here are the quick highlights.*

SECTION HIGHLIGHTS: YOUR *WHO*

"The ultimate value of life depends upon
awareness and the power of contemplation
rather than upon mere survival."

— ARISTOTLE

Your *Who* Highlights

- Your *Who* is the starting point for all your ideas, actions, and beliefs. If you're ever in a slump, it's because you're living your life inconsistently with your *Who*, your most important core value.
- If you feel held back because of people judging you, it's because you don't know who you are or what you stand for.
- Your *Who* is your rock.
- Having clarity over who you are is your source of power.
- I've never seen someone's *Who* be something negative. Humans are built to serve. We're good at the core.
- *"Whether you believe you can do a thing or not, you are right."* (Henry Ford)

- There has to be something that's more important to you than money.
- Most people would rather escape from their challenges by entertaining themselves instead of fixing their problems by educating themselves.
- Your parents and family are actually trying to support you. They just are running on a different operating system.
- What keeps couples together? Shared values. You don't need to have the exact same Who, but they need to be related.
- The greater your unhappiness, the greater your actions will need to be.
- *"The chains of habit are too light to be felt until they are too heavy to be broken."*
- You've been running your entire life with your hands tied behind your back, and it's time to explode forward.
- Your *Who* is what you would tell your younger self if you had the chance.
- Self-awareness and the boldness to follow through is the greatest gift you can give yourself.
- *"You are what you think all day long."* (Ralph Waldo Emerson)
- If you're not consistent in your bold thinking, you won't be consistent in your bold actions.
- If every day you woke up and felt the strength and boldness of your *Who*, your life would look dramatically different one year from today.
- I watched videos to get pulled up by people who #Believed more than me. I injected myself with #Believe vitamin C daily so if mediocrity sneezed on me, I wouldn't get sick.
- Proximity is power.

STEP 2

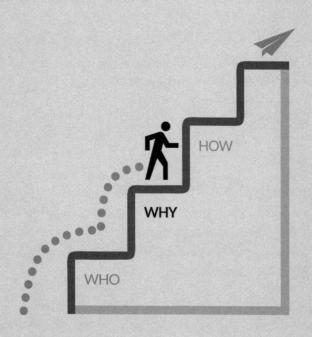

HOW

WHY

WHO

YOUR WHY

YOUR *WHY* = YOUR PURPOSE

"The climb might be tough and challenging, but the view is worth it. There is a purpose for that pain; you just can't always see it right away."

—VICTORIA ARLEN

Your purpose comes from your pain.

Think about the most painful moment you had to go through in your life—the moment that you'd never want to have to repeat, the moment where you felt the most worthless as a human being. Yep. That moment. It sucks, right?

Your purpose is to help other people who are currently facing the same struggle you went through.

That's it. It's that simple, and it's true. Whatever you went through that made you feel worthless is the seed of your purpose. Helping others who are currently facing those same challenges will fill you up. And they'll fill you up for life. This isn't just a purpose for this year. Helping people through that pain will never get old for you. How you do it (Step 3) will change with time, but the joy you get by helping these specific people will never get boring. You'll love it forever.

Entrepreneurs often have a hard time finding their purpose, their _Why_.

We're optimistic. We're positive. We're building a better future. We're changing the way things are done. We don't have time to sit and wallow in our past pains. What good will it do us? We have businesses to build. Let's go! We don't want to remember the negative because we want to stay in the land of positivity. And so we shut off and try to forget what happened so we can focus on building something better.

But not doing that deeper work is the exact thing that's holding back your success.

You can't do anything great without having had some great pain. Think of the people who achieve the most, your heroes, whoever they are—chances are they started with less than what you currently have right now. They had to endure a crazy amount of pain and suffering, and that pain drove them to succeed. Think of someone who you look up to as a leader in your industry, someone who changed the way things are done. Now, research their story. Understand where they came from. They suffered somewhere. And they turned that suffering into something amazing. I'm not suggesting that you live in the pain. I don't think that's healthy. But you do have to identify it. Your _Why_, the reason you get up in the morning when you're tired and have so many reasons not to get up and push, is rooted in a major pain that you experienced.

What kind of pain am I talking about?

PHYSICAL VS. PSYCHOLOGICAL PAIN

"He who has a why to live for can bear
almost any how."

—FRIEDRICH NIETZSCHE

Not all pain is created equal.

Physical pain is defined as "an unpleasant sensory and emotional experience associated with actual or potential tissue damage, or described in terms of such damage." Basically something happened to you that hurt your body. It may leave a physical scar, but your body heals, and you move on.

Psychological pain is different.

It's defined as "a lasting, unsustainable, and unpleasant feeling resulting from negative appraisal of an inability or deficiency of the self." Something happened to make you feel bad about yourself, and it's not going away. Some common causes of psychological pain are guilt, rejection, grief, loneliness, failure, embarrassment, shame, hurt feelings, jealousy, and trauma.

Psychological pain is more powerful.

If you get robbed at knifepoint and the thief accidentally gives you a minor cut to your arm while stealing your watch, your body will heal. Sure, it may scar, but after a few days your body has stopped hurting. The psychological scar, though, may last a lifetime. You may never want to walk alone again. You may develop a massive distrust of strangers. You may get anxious every time you look at a watch. You may stress out every time you see a knife. The psychological pain caused from that trauma can manifest in many different ways. The bottom line is, your body has healed but your mind has not.

So how do you heal it?

Some people say that time heals all wounds. And yes, with time the pain will numb, but time alone doesn't heal. Some advocate for meditation and mindfulness to reduce anxiety. It's a great immediate strategy to lower stress, but the stress will return. Others take a darker path and turn to drugs and alcohol to detach from the pain. I believe that ultimately the best path isn't away but through. The long-term solution is to turn that negative situation into a life-changing gift for yourself and others, to live a service life instead of a surface life, to give yourself a powerful reason to wake up every morning and work on building something better for yourself and the people around you.

I believe you are built to serve.

"If you want happiness for an hour, take a nap. If you want happiness for a day, go fishing. If you want happiness for a year, inherit a fortune. If you want happiness for a life-time, help somebody."

-CHINESE PROVERB

YOU ARE BUILT TO SERVE

"The best way to find yourself is to lose yourself
in the service of others."

—MAHATMA GANDHI

If you're not happy, it's because you're not serving.

There is a Chinese proverb that goes, "If you want happiness for
an hour, take a nap. If you want happiness for a day, go fishing.
If you want happiness for a year, inherit a fortune. If you want
happiness for a lifetime, help somebody." That's what I want for
you: a lifetime of happiness. To get out of the short-term trap of
thinking that getting that raise, buying that car, going on that
vacation, or getting more followers on social media will actually
make you happy.

This thought has been echoed for generations.

Saint Francis of Assisi said, "For it is in giving that we receive."
Leo Tolstoy said, "The sole meaning of life is to serve humanity."
Winston Churchill said, "We make a living by what we get;
we make a life by what we give." Muhammad Yunus said,
"Making money is happiness; making other people happy is

superhappiness." Every religion focuses on the importance of charity, service, and helping others. But it's also backed up by science.

Serving others is hardwired into our brain.

Functional magnetic resonance imaging (fMRI) measures brain activity. It detects changes in blood flow to know when a region of the brain is being used. Through fMRI scientific experiments, we know that serving others activates the same part of the brain that is stimulated by food and sex. Helping others is pleasurable. It's hardwired in us.

So whom do you help?

There are lots of people you can help. There are so many great causes out there. The whole world needs help in a million different ways. Why are you going to pick one group of people over another? Why one cause over another? The help that will resonate most with you comes from your pain, your story. The people who are currently facing the same pain that you experienced will be the ones you are drawn to most. And they will resonate with you as well because they see in you someone who went through it. You represent hope to them. Even if you don't have all the answers yet, you're a symbol that it's possible to make progress. Your purpose, your *Why* is to help them. You will become a mentor to them and, in that process, turn your weakest point in life into your greatest strength.

It's time for you to become a superhero.

YOU'RE A SUPERHERO

"Heroes are made by the path they choose, not the powers they are graced with."

—TONY STARK (IRON MAN)

Kal-El...

Was born on the planet Krypton and as a baby was sent to Earth just before his planet was destroyed. He became Superman and started protecting his new home, Earth. When his biological cousin Kara Zor-El was also sent to Earth, he helped her develop her powers and protect humanity as Supergirl. The helpless became the protectors.

Bruce Wayne...

Witnessed his parents being brutally murdered in front of him as a child. He became Batman to avenge his parents' death and bring justice to his city of Gotham. The victim became the enforcer.

Tony Stark...

Was a business magnate and scientist who got kidnapped and suffered a serious chest injury. His captors wanted him to build a weapon of mass destruction. Instead he created a powerful suit of armor that saved his life and allowed him to escape. He became Iron Man and used his suit to protect the world. The captive became the savior.

Steve Rogers...

Was a skinny, weak student who wanted to join the army to fight the Nazis but was rejected for being too frail. He was recruited for the secret super-soldier government project, which turned him into Captain America, a near perfect human with peak strength, stamina, and smarts. The weak became the strong.

Notice a pattern? It was their pain, suffering, and weakness that ultimately determined their powerful path forward. They chose to do something about that pain and turned it into a purposeful life that served others. They couldn't change the past, but they could use it as motivation to make the present and future better. And in that process they found fulfillment. Even though it was dangerous. Even though it was scary. Even though they had to fight against incredible odds. They got up every day and fought for good because that's their purpose. You can too. The massive pain that you went through isn't a black mark that will forever hold you back. It's the greatest gift of all time. It's the seed that will unlock your superpowers, if you're willing to accept it and grow from it.

Because you're not just a superhero, you're a tree.

YOU'RE A TREE

"All things share the same breath—the beast,
the tree, the man...the air shares its spirit with
all the life it supports."

—CHIEF SEATTLE

I think leaders are trees.

What does a tree do? A tree breathes in carbon dioxide, which is poison for people. A tree then eats it, grows from it, and spits out oxygen positivity for the world. That's your job as a leader. Your job is to face the pain, eat it, grow from it, and then create positivity and oxygen for others around you.

Comfort is the enemy of greatness.

When you're comfortable, you don't get strong. When you have plenty of fresh air and no adversity you crumble as soon as something gets hard. It's rarely the kids of rich parents who go on to do great things even though they have all the advantages that money, connections, and education can buy. Why is that? Because they're too comfortable. People who are comfortable don't create great things.

Your pain is your strength.

This is the fundamental mindset shift that most people never make but is required for success. The pain that you went through, that you're trying to forget...it's your strength. It's the way through. It's your answer. That pain is how you become the tree. You've experienced the pain, grown from it, are stronger now, and are able to help others who need the support. Be the tree, even if you feel like you don't know how.

You don't have all the answers yet.

One of the biggest barriers blocking you from becoming a tree is self doubt. "Who am I to be the expert?" you might think. "I don't have all the answers." And you're right—no one does. You're still on your journey. But just the fact that you're out there trying is an inspiration to others, and you also know more now than you did when you started. Think about the person you were five years ago. Think about how much you've grown since then. Could you give that person some advice that would be helpful? I bet you could! There are lots of people right now who are facing the difficulties you faced five years ago. That's who you're helping. And even if you're not completely done facing your fears and insecurities, you don't have to pretend that you are. That vulnerability actually makes you more relatable. Just know that you can still help. You have knowledge. You can inspire. You can spit out positivity for the world. You're a tree.

Oprah Winfrey is one of my favorite examples of a tree.

OPRAH WINFREY IS A TREE

"Turn your wounds into wisdom."

—OPRAH WINFREY

Here are a few things you may not know about Oprah's story:

- She was born Orpah, a Biblical name, but because people had such difficulty spelling and pronouncing it, they called her Oprah.
- Her unmarried parents separated soon after her birth, and she was raised mostly by her maternal grandmother on a farm in rural Mississippi.
- Her grandmother was a maid who told Oprah that she would also grow up to become a maid.
- She wore potato sacks as clothes because her grandmother couldn't afford to buy her real clothes. She was called "Sack Girl" in her community.
- She then went to live with her mom in an extremely poor and dangerous Milwaukee ghetto.
- Starting at nine years old, she was sexually abused by multiple family members, eventually becoming pregnant at age fourteen. She considered suicide.

- *"I hit rock-bottom. I became pregnant and hid the pregnancy. I'd intended to kill myself actually. I thought there's no way other than killing myself. I was just planning on how to do it. If I'd had the Internet, I might not be alive because now you can just Google how to do it."*
  (Oprah Winfrey)

It's hard to imagine a more challenging upbringing than what Oprah faced. For her to overcome that and become one of the wealthiest and most influential people in the world shows what is possible for people who grow through their pain.

If Oprah didn't go through that massive pain, she wouldn't be who she is today. The size and importance of your purpose comes in direct proportion to the size and importance of the pain you went through.

Your pain will define you. Either you succumb to it and give up, or you become a tree and allow people who are going through that pain to feel like they can breathe and that there is hope.

Let's talk about another tree, Mothers Against Drunk Driving (M.A.D.D.) founder Candy Lightner.

THE CANDY LIGHTNER STORY

"I started M.A.D.D. to deal with the issue
of drunk driving."

—CANDY LIGHTNER

On September 5, 1980, Candace Lightner's thirteen-year-old daughter, Cari, was killed by a drunk driver.
Cari was walking with a friend to a church carnival in Fair Oaks, California. Out of nowhere, a car hit Cari with a force so hard that she was knocked out of her shoes and flew 125 feet. She died shortly after the accident. The driver who hit Cari never stopped the car. He just drove off.

It was later learned that the driver was drunk when the accident happened, and it wasn't his first drunk-driving accident. Police told Candace that the driver would likely receive little punishment for killing her daughter.

Massive. Pain.

But instead of succumbing to it, Candace used that pain as fuel to create change. Four days after her daughter died, Candace started Mothers Against Drunk Drivers (later changed to Mothers

Against Drunk Driving). It was a grassroots organization to advocate for harsher legal penalties for drunk driving.

Up until that point, Candace was a divorced mom of three and a real estate agent. She had no interest in social issues or politics. "I wasn't even registered to vote," she told People magazine.

Today M.A.D.D. has at least one office in every state in America and every province in Canada. They claim that drunk driving has been cut in half since M.A.D.D. was founded.

Candace became a tree.

It would have been easy for her to fall into depression after the loss of her daughter. Everyone would have understood. Most people probably would have expected it. But instead of allowing herself to be poisoned by the pain, she grew from it and created an organization that has saved countless lives. A divorced mom of three who worked as a real-estate agent and wasn't even registered to vote became a hero.

Your purpose comes from your pain.

Let me tell you about my pain and the worst day of my life.

THE WORST DAY OF MY LIFE

"I was tired of being broke. I was tired of eating the
same bean salad lunch every day because it was cheap
and would fill me up."

—EVAN CARMICHAEL

I just told my business partner, "I quit."

I was tired of not making money. I was tired of things not
working. I was tired of getting up every day, putting in effort, and
not seeing any results. I would understand if I was slacking off or
not taking it seriously, but I was giving everything I had, and we
had no momentum. So at a family dinner, I went upstairs, called
my partner, and told him, "I quit."

And then I cried. A lot.

I cried so much that I wasn't sure what was coming out of my
eyes and what was coming out of my nose. Then my mom came
upstairs, put her hand on my shoulder, and tried to console me.
But I had no idea what she was saying. I was too lost. I couldn't
believe I had just quit on something I deeply cared about. It was
anti-#Believe (even though I didn't know what my *Who* was
back then). It wasn't who I was.

69

But I was so tired.

I was tired of being broke. I was tired of eating the same bean-salad lunch every day because it was cheap and would fill me up. I was tired of telling my friends that I couldn't go out with them at night because I was "hustling and living the entrepreneur life," meanwhile I was making $300 per month and couldn't afford the twenty dollars it would cost me for the evening's pizza and beer. I was tired of celebrating a win with McDonald's French fries because I couldn't afford to have the whole meal.

I could have done better.

I honestly made it harder on myself than it needed to be. I could have told my friends I didn't have any money. We could have done something else that was free. I was just too embarrassed and ashamed. And so I went inwards. I isolated myself, which made the entrepreneur journey so much harder.

Quitting on my business partner was the worst day of my life. I went to bed that night having no idea what I was going to do. I had turned down huge jobs with big paydays to do this. And now I was quitting. What was I supposed to do next? That pain became my *Why*—helping entrepreneurs not feel as defeated, alone, and hopeless as I felt.

My pain led to my purpose.

When my first book,
***Your One Word**, came
out, my wife and I went
to McDonald's to cele-
brate as a throwback
to my early days as an
entrepreneur. This time
I got an entire meal,
not just the fries.*

MY PURPOSE IS TO HELP ENTREPRENEURS

"When you find your purpose, it gives you the strength
to do things that you never thought were possible."

—EVAN CARMICHAEL

When I'm helping entrepreneurs I forget everything.

I forget to sleep. I forget to eat. I forget to go to the bathroom.
I forget everything. It's just you and me. I'm totally zoned in.
Because I want to help you. I sometimes need to save myself from
myself. I was once speaking at a conference in Los Angeles. It was
a four-day event where I only went to three sessions (my speech
and the two speeches put on by the organizers and a friend of
mine). The rest of the time I was in the hotel lobby helping entrepreneurs. I woke up at 7:30 a.m. and went to the lobby and stayed
there until 2:30 the next morning, stopping once for a food and
bathroom break, which consisted of going to Subway to grab a
sandwich and then back to the hotel lobby to help more.

I loved it, but it wasn't healthy.

The lack of rest, water, and food caught up to me quickly. I was
running a fever all four days but never noticed—not until I left

the entrepreneurs and went back to my hotel room. It wasn't healthy, but I wanted to help so much that I couldn't stop. I knew that last twenty-minute session with the latest entrepreneur was impactful, so I kept going.

Your purpose will keep you going.

I'm an introvert who hates the spotlight. Yet I've spoken all around the world, and my videos have reached hundreds of millions of people. It's wild. How is that possible? When you find your purpose, it gives you the strength to do things you never thought were possible. It gives you new courage because you're on a mission.

I also had no natural talent for this.

I used to ask my sister to come into my office, make sure my camera was in focus, press the record button, and then leave the room. I couldn't record with her (or anyone) in the room because I was too nervous. It took me 350 videos before I wasn't completely embarrassed by my own content. It wasn't until I passed the 700 video mark that I actually inspired myself, that I finally felt like I was kind of getting good at this video thing. Over 700 videos! Most people would have quit way sooner. And it's not because I'm superhuman. I'm not. I'm just like you. But I stuck with it because it was my purpose. I had to do it. I had to overcome the obstacles. Otherwise I wouldn't be able to serve and help entrepreneurs. My *Why* keeps me going. It gets me out of bed when I'm tired. It keeps me pushing when I'm afraid.

What happens if you haven't been through any pain?

A PAIN-FREE LIFE?

"We have the tendency to run away from suffering
and to look for happiness. But, in fact,
if you have not suffered, you have no chance
to experience real happiness."

—THICH NHAT HANH

I received a message from a fan that surprised me.

He said, "Evan, you say your purpose comes from your pain. I haven't really experienced any great pain in my life. Can I still build something great?"

My honest answer is...I don't know.

I can tell you that I've never seen it. Of all the successful people I've studied, I've never seen anyone have massive success without having a lot of pain in their life. It's why the kids of rich people rarely do great things. Most of them haven't suffered much. Everything was handed to them. Life was too comfortable. Perhaps their real suffering is never proving themselves and living in the shadow of their family. I tend to agree with Thich Nhat Hanh's quote from above: "If you have not suffered... you have no chance to experience real happiness."

Ok, then can you force pain on yourself?

You can. But oh boy is it hard to do. Doing something just because it's painful is not something we're wired to do. What I'd suggest, if you haven't experienced great pain, is to work daily to expand your comfort zone. When you get an idea for something that scares you, go do it. Train yourself so that as soon as you come up with a thought for something you'd like to try and it makes you nervous, you need to go do it. It's not just randomly putting yourself in painful situations, but rather listening to your intuition with the thoughts that are already coming to you, and finding a way to get started on them.

You were not meant to photocopy your day over and over again.

If you have no pain, you're living a life fully inside your comfort zone, and that's not a recipe for fulfillment. So pay attention to your ideas, trust that they are right for you, and try them out, especially when they make you nervous. As you blast through your comfort zone, you'll find pain and begin the process of discovering your purpose.

If you feel fulfilled, I have nothing for you.

If you have no pain and don't want something more out of your life, I'm pumped for you. I haven't met that person though.

What about compassion fatigue? Can you serve too much?

COMPASSION FATIGUE

"Compassion Fatigue is a state experienced by those helping people or animals in distress; it is an extreme state of tension and preoccupation with the suffering of those being helped to the degree that it can create a secondary traumatic stress for the helper."

— DR. CHARLES FIGLEY

Another fan wrote in with an interesting question:

"Evan, you say humans are built to serve. That your happiness comes from serving others. What about compassion fatigue? You spend so much time helping others that you don't look after yourself?"

Compassion fatigue is real.

I already told you about the story of me in Los Angeles, sitting in the hotel lobby helping entrepreneurs, barely sleeping, not eating, and running a fever for four days. While I was in the zone, I didn't notice that my body was falling apart. If I had stayed there for another week, I probably would have just collapsed in the middle of a meeting while helping an entrepreneur. It wasn't smart, but I couldn't help it.

Balance is key.

When I got on the flight back to Toronto I thought to myself, *Wow that was amazing! It's crazy how many people I helped and how meaningful the impact was on them.* I need to find a way to keep doing this. *But it has to be a way that doesn't kill me. Otherwise I'm of no use to anyone.* So I started a daily routine of helping an entrepreneur every morning. It's once a day instead of all day. I set up a routine and schedule to save me from myself. If you suffer from compassion fatigue, then you need to figure out what balance looks like for you and create a schedule that supports it.

But it's not the norm.

While compassion fatigue is very real, it's not the norm. Could you imagine a world where everyone gave so much of themselves that they started to burn out? If that were the biggest problem we face as society, then we'd be living in a pretty amazing world. Unfortunately, most people have no idea what their *Why* is. Most people don't know how they should be serving others. Most people are burning out because they're not living their purpose.

Now let's find your Why. You're ready.

I'm twenty-two here. I just sold my business and am graduating from the University of Toronto. I have no idea what I want to do next. The guy next to me looks pretty happy though.

Later that same year I got invited to represent Canada at the APEC Young Leaders Forum in Mexico. It was the start of my international speaking career. I miss that hair!

WHAT'S YOUR *WHY?*

"There is no greater gift you can give or receive than to honor your calling. It's why you were born. And how you become most truly alive."

—OPRAH WINFREY

Do you know what the most painful moment of your life is?

Some people know it immediately. They can see it in their mind right now. It's terrible and they never want to go back. Others don't know what the most painful moment of their life is. It's a hard question. These next three exercises will help give you more clarity. They will help you find your *Why*, and from there we can build an amazing future for you.

Exercise #1. Ten-Year Chunking

Here we divide your life into ten-year chunks, figure out what the most painful moments were, and find their common elements to give you clarity on your purpose.

Exercise #2. Emotional Patterns

Here we look at the most common causes of psychological pain and how they have shown up in your life.

Exercise #3. Police Lineup

Here we look at the people who have caused the most pain in your life and figure out what your purpose is through them.

Ready? Pull out your worksheets (see the start of this book to get them for free), or grab some paper and let's get started!

TEN-YEAR CHUNKING

> "Ten years ago, I still feared loss enough to abandon myself in order to keep things stable. I'd smile when I was sad, pretend to like people who appalled me. What I now know is that losses aren't cataclysmic if they teach the heart and soul."
>
> —MARTHA BECK

How old are you right now?

On a piece of paper, divide your life into ten-year chunks. For example, at the time of this writing I'm thirty-nine years old. So I'd divide my page into four chunks that would read:

- 29–39
- 19–29
- 9–19
- 0–9

Do it for your age. Now let's do some time traveling.

Close your eyes and start with the most recent decade. Think about what you've been through and the experiences you've had. If you're a positive, optimistic person, it's easy to lean in on gratitude and how much you've learned and grown in the past decade. That's amazing, but not for this exercise. We need to get to your pain. Think about the worst thing that happened to you. When did you feel most worthless as a human in the past decade? With your eyes closed, try to go back and experience it again. Put yourself there. Feel how it feels. Then open your eyes and write down one sentence about the experience and three descriptive keywords for how it made you feel. For example, maybe it was being fired by your boss. So you would write: "I was fired from my job." And the descriptive keywords might look like: "Failure, Rejection, Useless."

Repeat this exercise for every ten-year chunk on your page.

The more chunks you have, the more history you have to pull from. Also, if you can't fill one out, don't worry. For example, if you're twenty-one you might have a memory from eleven to twenty-one, and from one to eleven, but nothing from zero to one. Totally normal. I don't remember what happened to me when I was a one-year-old either!

What's the common thread?

Look at your three descriptive keywords. What's common between your ten-year chunks? What's the recurring theme? This is the starting point of your *Why*.

If you didn't find it yet, don't worry; let's check in on your emotional patterns.

EMOTIONAL PATTERNS

"Pattern recognition is very important
to solve the Cube."

—ERNO RUBIK

You have emotional patterns that trigger your pain.

On a new page, write the following words down with space to write beside and underneath them:

- Guilt
- Rejection
- Grief
- Loneliness
- Failure
- Embarrassment
- Shame
- Hurt feelings
- Jealousy
- Trauma

Next to each word write down three times in your life when you felt each one. Just write a quick note to remind yourself of the moment. For example, under failure I would write, "My first business." Try to come up with three examples for each word.

You'll find two things start to happen.

The first is that some words will be very easy to find three examples for, while others will take a lot of thinking. You may not even be able to come up with three at all. This gives you insight into where your pain lies. For example, if you have lots of examples of loneliness but not many examples of grief, then there's a good chance that your *Why* will have something to do with helping people not feel lonely. The second is you'll find the same experience shows up for multiple categories. For example, I'd put my first business under guilt, rejection, loneliness, failure, embarrassment, shame, and hurt feelings. That's seven of the ten categories! It's no wonder it's such a painful moment from my life. Any experience that shows up under multiple categories gives you a sense of how intense that painful memory was for you. And the more intense it was, the more likely it's the foundation for your purpose.

Are we getting closer? It's not a fun trip going into your painful past, but it is very illuminating, and I promise it'll take you to a positive place you never even knew existed.

Here is one last exercise for you to try: the police lineup.

EMOTIONAL PATTERNS THAT TRIGGER PAIN

"Let's not forget that the little emotions are the great captains of our lives and we obey them without realizing it." - Vincent Van Gogh

- GUILT
- REJECTION
- GRIEF
- LONELINESS
- FAILURE
- EMBARRASSMENT
- SHAME
- HURT
- JEALOUSY
- TRAUMA

POLICE LINEUP

"The more successful the villain,
the more successful the picture."

—ALFRED HITCHCOCK

Have you ever seen those movies...

Where they line up a criminal suspect with people who look like them, and then an eyewitness has to say who committed the crime? It's a police lineup, and we're going to use it for the villains in your life.

Think about the biggest villains in your life.

The people who hurt you the most. The ones who caused you the most pain. The ones you wish never came into your life. The ones you wouldn't wish on anybody you love. Now make a list of them. You need to find at least one and at most five. Others might come to mind, but keep it to the worst five. Put them into your own police lineup by writing their names on a fresh piece of paper.

Now let's apply emotional patterns to them.

Next to each of the people on your list, write down the one thing they did that was the most painful to you and how it made you feel. You can pull from our existing list: guilt, rejection, grief, loneliness, failure, embarrassment, shame, hurt feelings, jealousy, and trauma. If none of those describe how you felt when they caused you so much pain, add your own words.

Your purpose is to be the opposite of your police lineup.

However these villains made you feel, your *Why* will be to help other people feel the exact opposite. If they made you feel shame, you'll want to make people feel proud. If they made you feel like a failure, you'll want to make people feel like winners. If they made you feel guilt, you'll want to help people feel acceptance.

The villains in your police lineup are out of time.

You may have lived your life in fear, pain, and suffering at the hands of these people. Little did they know that something amazing is about to come from it—that they created a new superhero who is now on a quest to save the world and eradicate their ability to hurt people ever again. Their time is over. It's going to be okay for people to live in the open again without fear, because you're going to make it that way.

Need an example? Let's look at Aleks again, the salsa-school entrepreneur I invested in.

FINDING ALEKS'S WHY

"Help the vulnerable people who are alone and lost
have a place where they can belong."

—ALEKS SAIYAN

**Ten-Year Chunking (Aleks is thirty-three years old
at the time of this writing)**

- Age 23–33: "Realizing I shouldn't be with my
  fiancé" → failure, quitter, hopeless.
- Age 13–23: "Walking during recess and thinking I will
  always be alone" → not accepted, rejected, worthless.
- Age 3–13: "Hearing my cousin get beaten by his father as
  punishment" → weak, helpless, vulnerable.
- Age 0–3: "Can't remember."

Recurring theme: Help the vulnerable people who are alone and
lost have a place where they can belong.

Emotional Patterns

- **Guilt**
  - Didn't walk back to defend my mom.
  - Couldn't help my brother when I was younger.
  - Took too long to stop being a kid in my business.

- **Rejection**
  - First girl I asked out in grade five.
  - The instructors who didn't believe in me.
  - Didn't get into university.

- **Grief**
  - My brother slipping up.
  - My mom having cancer.
  - Finding out what my dad did.

- **Loneliness**
  - High school, walking alone outside.
  - Coming home to an empty house.
  - Breaking up after my five-year relationship.

- **Failure**
  - Didn't get into university.
  - People complaining about my classes.
  - Instructors quitting my school.

- **Embarrassment**
  - Made mistakes in a dance performance.
  - Dancing with my own dance instructor and making mistakes.
  - Teaching my first classes and sucking at it.

- **Shame**
  - Wasn't smart enough to help my brother.
  - Didn't work hard enough to get into university right away.
  - Avoiding my responsibilities but still getting support from my family.

- **Hurt feelings**
  - Being yelled at by a girl I had a crush on.
  - Finding out why my mom left my dad.
  - Being lied to by my brother.

- **Jealousy**
  - My ex dancing too close with other guys in bachata.
  - My mom giving more attention to my brother.
  - My mentor, capable of helping others more than me.

- **Trauma**
  - Breaking my arm.
  - Finding out my mom has cancer.
  - My brother making old mistakes again.

Police Lineup

- Samia: made me feel worthless (loneliness, rejection, embarrassment, hurt feelings).
- Giora: made me feel like I don't belong (loneliness, rejection, embarrassment, hurt feelings).

I profiled Aleks in the *Who* part of this book as well. His *Who* is #Belong. He cares about self-acceptance, understanding, and being a hero. Now you get to see his most painful moments in his life that make up his *Why*. Can you see how this all connects? Aleks now runs Toronto Dance Salsa, a purpose driven business that doesn't just teach people how to dance salsa, but makes people feel like they #Belong. Through his *Who* and his *Why* he is impacting thousands of people and building a successful company in the process.

Now it's time to turn your pain into something that will help people.

*Aleks's **Who** is #Belong. Mine is #Believe. When you know your **Who** and your **Why**, it allows you to build an impactful business that can touch the lives of millions of people.*

WHO SPECIFICALLY WILL YOU HELP?

"No problem can be solved until it is reduced to some simple form. The changing of a vague difficulty into a specific, concrete form is a very essential element in thinking."

—J.P. MORGAN

You don't want to serve everyone equally.

You just went through three painful exercises. Now it's time to do something positive with that pain. You need to get specific on who you're going to help, and that will come from the specific pains and circumstances you faced.

For example, if your top pain was shame, you'll want to help people feel proud. And yes, helping anybody feel proud will make you feel amazing. But specifically, helping people who are battling the same thing you battled will fill you up to another level. If it was your teachers who made you feel shame, then you'll love trying to reform the education system and making students feel proud. Because that was you. You're helping everyone who is currently facing what you faced. We need to create a profile of the specific people you want to help most. There are a few ways to go about this.

Based on type of pain:

- Rejection, grief, loneliness, failure, embarrassment, shame, hurt feelings, jealousy, trauma.
- Example: Brené Brown created multiple best-selling books and popular videos around shame because she struggled with how people perceived her.

Based on demographics:

- Age, gender, ethnicity, income, religion, sexual orientation, marital status, geographic area, language.
- Example: Oprah Winfrey does a lot of work supporting the black community, women, and the underprivileged, because she faced discrimination.

Based on interests:

- Industry, sports, politics, activities, hobbies, education, clubs, beliefs, life choices.
- Example: I want to help entrepreneurs because of how much I struggled in my first business and how the failures impacted my self-esteem.

There's no right or wrong here. There's just right or wrong for you. There are lots of good causes out there. But they aren't all meant for you. Helping rescue animals is somebody's purpose. It comes from their pain. It doesn't mean you hate dogs if you don't get involved. You just have a different calling, and that's what you need to pursue.

Let's create your ideal target persona.

YOUR IDEAL TARGET PERSONA

"My persona has always been what a man
was never supposed to be.
Outrageous, gregarious, crazy, silly, funny."

—RICHARD SIMMONS

'Persona' is a marketing term.

It's a semi-fictional representation of your ideal target audience, based on motivations, demographics, and interests. We're going to figure out how to use your story to specifically identify your ideal target persona.

Look at the categories on the previous page.

Then see which specific ones match your story. For example, I've already shared from the pain category that I'd put my first business under guilt, rejection, loneliness, failure, embarrassment, shame, and hurt feelings. I've got a lot of pain that I can cover. Next, if I go to demographics, the most relevant ones are income and age. I had no money and hated it. I was also young and felt insecure about my age. I still like helping older entrepreneurs who have a lot of money, but it's not part of my story. The other demographics don't apply. Sure, I'm a white male from Canada who is straight and married, but those don't apply to my story, so I'd just as easily connect with a Japanese lesbian. You need to figure out which demographics matter to your story. Finally, in the interests category, the only thing that really matters for me is entrepreneurs. I don't care about your hobbies, sports affiliation, clubs, life choices, etc. So knowing that combination of pain points, demographics, and interests helps me define the persona that I'm targeting for all of my products, services, and marketing.

Now it's your turn.

Take out your worksheets or a piece of paper, and go through the same exercise I just demonstrated. Go back to the most painful moment in your life and think about which pain points that moment hit on. Think about the demographics that matter to you for the types of people your pain will serve. Then finish off with the interests that make a difference. Again, it's not judging or comparing. It doesn't mean you'll turn away people who need help. Many of the people in my audience aren't even entrepreneurs; they just like the #Believe message. I'll still help them when they come to my workshops or join my live streams. But it's not my core. It's not who I'm intentionally going after. You need to figure out who you are intentionally going after, and this exercise will give you that clarity. Take your time, go step by step, and refer back to this page every time you're creating a new product, service, or marketing campaign to remind yourself of what you're trying to accomplish and the people you are trying to serve. You're going to need it, because the next task might be the hardest thing you've ever done.

You need to tell your story publicly and become a leader.

BECOMING A LEADER

"The currency of leadership is transparency. You've got to be truthful. There are moments where you've got to share your soul and conscience with people and show them who you are, and not be afraid of it."

—HOWARD SCHULTZ

People connect with people.

The greatest asset you have is you. Your *Who* and your *Why* are unique. That's what makes you, you. And since people connect with people, you need to share your story so that your ideal target persona will connect with you.

I need to know that you understand *me.*

It's easy for people to give advice. Everybody has an opinion on what others should do. Why are you any different? Why should I listen to you? You don't know what I'm going through…Except you do! Because you went through the exact same thing. But unless you tell me what you went through, I'm not going to listen. If I don't feel like you *understand* me, that you're *just like* me, I'm tuning out.

You need to connect with people emotionally before you connect with them logically.

You can have all the greatest strategies in the world. People won't listen or follow them until they are emotionally invested. Your story, your *Who* and your *Why* is what will connect them. If you want to lose weight, you know how. Eat less. Eat healthier. Work out. Every weight loss plan is some variant of that. You know eating junk food means you'll gain weight. You know it, and yet you keep doing it because you're not emotionally invested in the people giving you the advice. They don't know what you're going through. They aren't facing the same problems. You don't know their story, so you don't end up following their advice.

Let's say you used to be a drug addict. You're clean now but substituted junk food for drugs, and now someone is offering you advice on how to lose weight. "You don't know me," you say. "Yeah, get rid of junk food. But if I do that, I'll go back to drugs. Your strategies might work for normal people, but not for me." But what if the person giving advice was a drug addict too, and also substituted food for drugs, and also gained a ton of weight, but then found a way through? They *are* like you.

You need to tell your story. You need to share your *Who* and your *Why* before others will listen to your *How*.

I know because Michael Edwards may have saved my brain.

SAVING EVAN'S BRAIN

"I know what it's like to go through a concussion
and I didn't want Evan to suffer as much as I did."

— MICHAEL EDWARDS

I broke my neck in two spots, compressed my upper back, and got a concussion.

It was on my 2019 tour. I went to twenty-three cities in ninety days, meeting entrepreneurs across America while fulfilling my promise to my wife to take her to every city in America with over a million people. But two months in, on my wife's birthday, something terrible happened. We were in Colorado, and I was researching some medical hacks. Sometimes I get a little queasy when I'm thinking about medical information. This time though, I fainted. I passed out in my chair, fell over, hit the front of my head against the wall, then the back of my head on the baseboard, which cut my head open. I was rushed to the hospital. I needed three staples for my head, and a neck brace for sixty days because I broke my neck and compressed my upper back. I also had a concussion, and having normal conversations was difficult. The doctors said there was a 50 percent chance I would need spinal surgery.

Holy cow, what just happened?

We went from having an amazing cross-country tour and getting ready to celebrate my wife's birthday to me suddenly being in the hospital and potentially needing spinal surgery. It was crazy. The pain was intense, but the worst part was the concussion. I'd never had a concussion before. Let me tell you, it sucks. I couldn't think clearly. I couldn't carry on a conversation. I couldn't even pull up my pants by myself. I didn't mind that as much. I didn't mind the pain either. But not thinking properly, for me, was devastating.

My community sprung to action.

I let my community know what had happened and immediately people wrote in. Most offered prayers, good wishes, and love. Some offered generic support—*If there's anything I can do to help, just let me know*—and others offered specific advice. I was recommended all kinds of books, pills, doctors, videos, therapies, foods, sprays, meditations, songs, podcasts, and so on. It was all out of love, and it was overwhelming, especially for someone with a concussion who couldn't think clearly. I didn't know what to do. Neither did my wife, Nina. We were in Colorado, miles away from our home and our support network in Toronto. I'd never fainted before, had never broken anything that needed a cast before, and had never had a concussion before.

And then "The Concussion Man," Michael Edwards messaged me.

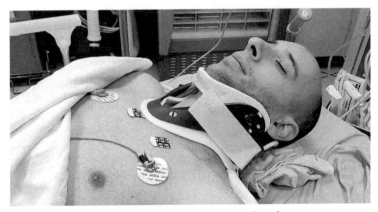

*Me in the hospital in Colorado after breaking my neck and getting
a concussion.*

*I finished the rest of my workshop tour in pain, but quickly healed from my
concussion.*

THE CONCUSSION MAN

"I knew I couldn't live in this pain anymore. And I knew
the doctors couldn't help so I began to take it upon
myself and become my own doctor."

—MICHAEL EDWARDS

I met Michael in Indianapolis a month prior to my injury.

We almost didn't meet. Indianapolis doesn't have a million
people in it, and that was my criteria for visiting cities, but the
greater Indianapolis area did, so my wife and I decided we'd go.
Michael almost didn't come either. He drove four hours from
Kentucky to get to my event because he was a fan of my content
and wanted to meet me.

Michael has suffered four concussions and was told by
doctors he'd never recover. His first concussion came at age two
when his cousin hit him in the back of the head with a metal
baseball bat. Then at fifteen, after being locked in a locker and
forced to fight, he got his second concussion and was suspended
from school. The next day he smacked his head on a hayfork in
the same spot the bully had hit him, and he had a second-impact
concussion. At nineteen, he was assaulted on the street, hit his

head on the concrete and suffered another concussion. To make matters worse, his father traumatized him, his doctors told him he'd never recover, and he tried to commit suicide.

But Michael refused to give up:

"I knew I couldn't live in this pain anymore. And I knew the doctors couldn't help so I began to take it upon myself and become my own doctor. Researching and experimenting with different cocktails of supplements and using food as medicine to reverse the damage. I thought at the very least I would die trying to save myself. But instead I started noticing positive change. Looking back on it, I believe it was a combination of leaving my toxic environment (I couldn't heal being in survival mode) and using food to heal my body. And when you notice something is working, you become obsessed with it, or at least I did. Although I was feeling better, I still felt plateaued in my healing. I tried some other alternative therapies with not much success, and then I decided to research and experiment with different arts of meditation. I had to reach deep brainwaves and reach my limbic system in order for any healing to occur. I did this by heightening emotions of appreciation, care, love, and certainty behind each closure of my meditations. I repeatedly visualized transforming into the healed version of me. When you are able to do this so well, your brain believes in the experience so strongly that it creates a neuropharmacy inside the body that heals itself."

Michael had been through four concussions and healed himself. He deeply understood the problem I was facing and the battle that was ahead for me.

So when Michael reached out, I paid attention.

GETTING PEOPLE'S ATTENTION

"Sharing my story was hard and very emotional for me.
I was nervous to do it."

—MICHAEL EDWARDS

Why Michael?

So many people offered advice. So many people wanted to help—people I've known for years, people I've had over to my house. Why listen to some guy I met for a couple of hours on a tour stop instead of listening to people much closer to me?

Because I knew his story.

When I met Michael, he told me about what had happened to him. I learned about his concussions and his amazing road to recovery. At the time, I just saw another entrepreneur who had done what was required to grow. He overcame adversity and now wanted to help others do the same. His purpose came from his pain. I had no need for his expertise, though, because I didn't have a concussion problem.

Until I did.

Here was a guy who overcame four concussions. People gave up on him. Doctors told him he wouldn't recover. But he didn't stop hacking his routine, mind-set, and brain until he found something that worked. He kept believing in his ability to recover, even when everyone else gave up on him.

I knew this because he shared his story.

Michael's a pretty shy guy. He's not the in-your-face, gregarious, outgoing type of entrepreneur. He's introverted, careful about his words, and doesn't crave the spotlight. But he shared his journey with me because his story has power. His story is what connected him to me. His story is what made me remember him. He hasn't gone off and helped millions of people (yet). At the time of this writing, he's trying to figure out how to turn his story and solution into a business that helps people heal themselves.

If Michael didn't share his story, I wouldn't have listened.

If he had found out about my concussion and just sent me a message giving me suggestions, he would have been lumped into the same category as everyone else who wrote in. He cares. I love it. But if I can't tell that he understands my situation, I'm likely not going to listen. But because I felt like he did understand me and had conquered an even greater battle than what I was facing, I was all ears.

And he convinced me to do something I never thought would work.

I NEVER THOUGHT I'D DO THIS

"Meditation creates a natural environment
for the body to heal itself."

—MICHAEL EDWARDS

Michael said I needed to do healing meditation.

Now, I fully believe in the benefits of meditation. I believe the science. I believe the people who tell me it works for them. But it never worked for me. I've tried following YouTube videos, guided meditation apps, and one-on-one coaching with some of the best meditation teachers in the world. But I never felt anything. I didn't feel any different coming out of a meditation than going in. I must have tried thirty to forty different techniques from different people, because I believe it works. I just never found the method that worked for me. And yet, the thing that never worked for me was the very thing my new advisor promised would heal me.

Great. I'm all in. Tell me what to do.

He gave me specific music to listen to, specific visualizations to do while meditating, specific instructions on how to position myself, specific instructions on timing and frequency. He followed up with me regularly and kept sending his support, belief, and guidance. When I loaded my messages, his was the first one I went to, because at this moment in my life he was one of the most important people around me.

I did the meditations because I believed in Michael.

And I believed in Michael because he told his story. Again, it comes back to his story. His journey got my attention. It got me to do something that I never had success with. I stuck with it. I did a morning and evening meditation every day, exactly like Michael had instructed me to. I didn't miss a single day. What was a "nice-to-have" luxury suddenly became a top priority because I needed to get rid of this concussion.

Then I started to heal.

Within a couple days, I started feeling better. I still had a lot of brain fog, but I could start to think again. One week later, I was able to lead a workshop for an hour and a half. Another week later, I could lead my full three-hour workshop. Two more weeks and I stopped getting dizzy when I lay down. The broken bone in my neck also healed. Was it because of my meditation, or just normal healing? I honestly don't know. But I was dedicated to my meditation because I wanted to heal like Michael had. He told his story and it impacted me. Now it's time for you to tell yours.

But telling your story is going to be scary.

Me and Michael Edwards in Indianapolis. This was taken a month before the accident that led to my concussion. I'm so glad he had the courage to share his story with me.

SHARING IS SCARY

"My story is a freedom song of struggle. It is about finding one's purpose, how to overcome fear and to stand up for causes bigger than one's self."

—CORETTA SCOTT KING

Most people aren't willing to share their story because they're afraid.

You're afraid of being judged. You're afraid of what people will say. You're afraid that people won't look at you the same way anymore. You were "normal" the day before, but now you're an ex-drug addict. Now you're someone who tried to commit suicide. Now you're someone who has depression or some disease or a disorder. Now you don't fit in anymore. And that's scary.

Remember that you're a tree.

You're a leader. You want to have an impact. You want to make a difference. This is how you do it. If you're afraid to share your story, then you'll never reach the people you can help. If you don't share your story, it just confirms for everyone like you that you *should* be ashamed and afraid, that this thing that happened to you and lots of other people *shouldn't* be talked about. Your silence perpetuates everyone's silence.

Until you're not silent.

Sharing your story gives hope to people who are suffering the same thing. It gives them permission to feel they're not alone. It gives them a promise of a better world, because now there's something they can do about it. They can act. They can change. They can grow. Because you're here. Even if you haven't figured it out yet. Even if you're still on your journey. You can help the person who you were five years ago, and there are lots of people who are exactly like the person you were five years ago. They need your voice. They need your guidance. They need your leadership.

Telling your story is scary.

But you do scary. You do difficult. You take on challenges. You don't want to just do what's safe, predictable, easy. You don't want to photocopy the same day of your life over and over again. This is what growth looks like. Pushing barriers, taking on your fears, getting to the next level. And then you can bring people with you and lift them up so they can grow as well. Otherwise, you'll get to the end of your life and realize that you could have done so much, but you played small because you were afraid. And that is not an acceptable outcome for your life. Not for you. You're a leader. You're a tree.

Here's my friend Mark Drager's story. He built a seven-figure business, and he's a tree too.

MARK'S STORY

"I can't shake that feeling of being the little boy who's
a waste of space. The feeling of not being good
enough is something I have to work on every day.
Every day I have something to prove."

—MARK DRAGER

It's hard for me to remember a time when
I felt comfortable.

*"As a kid I can remember these moments, memories of my heart
pumping in my ears so hard it would hurt, moments where I'd
have to stick up for myself but my voice would become shaky,
these times where I'd struggle to hold back the tears. And then the
detached feeling would come as the rest of the world blurred into
slow motion, and I could hear my own voice in my head—almost
having a conversation with myself. Later in life, I came to learn
that these are simply the side effects of fear, anger, and anxiety.
But as a kid growing up, I didn't know that. From the age of seven
onward I was raised in a home where I was always on edge, never
sure if what I said, or what I did, or how I acted would get me
into trouble. One moment everything was fine and the next I was
told I was the most ungrateful, worthless, and pathetic waste of*

space. And that's what comes from growing up with a manic, bitter, alcoholic stepfather. That was my home life until I moved out at sixteen. It took me a long time to get comfortable with my childhood and to understand how it shaped me into the person I am today. How the anxiety, the fear, and the constant feeling of never being good enough lead me to my ultimate purpose: to help people create #extraordinary businesses."

Fight the feeling of not being good enough.

"And so, as I write this, I have everything an outsider, even my friends, would see as indicators of success. At thirty-six, I'm a father of four amazing kids (ages six to thirteen). I've been with my wife for almost twenty years (yes, we're high-school sweethearts). I founded a marketing agency (Phanta.com) and over the past thirteen years have grown it from nothing to a multi-million dollar per year business. I have helped launch startups and transformed international brands...and yet, I still wake up every morning with the feeling that I have something to prove. Because I can't shake that feeling of being the little boy who's a waste of space. The feeling of not being good enough is something I have to work on every day. Every day I have something to prove: to my family, to my ex-coworkers, to my high school friends, to my staff, and to myself. I have to prove that I'm good enough."

My greatest hope for you.

"There used to come a time in client meetings when I'd have the overwhelming sensation to jump up and get down on my knees in front of the client and beg. The feeling would become so real that I'd almost have to hold myself back. Otherwise, there I would be, literally begging. Not for the business. Not for the money. For the opportunity to help them. Because more than anything, deep down I want to help people build the most extraordinary and meaningful things possible: a business, an experience—it doesn't matter. I love being a part of the process, as small as it may be, that leads to the moment when others look at what you've done and say, 'You did that?' Because I know what those of us with something to prove are capable of. You have the chance to build something that you're proud of. To do something that matters. And I can't wait to see what you do."

How does Mark's story help him get clients for PHANTA, his digital marketing agency?

THE MAN WITH SOMETHING TO PROVE

"We're not in this to simply produce a video or build a lead generation campaign—we're in this to show all those who doubt us how wrong they are."

—MARK DRAGER

Unlocking and living my purpose unlocks superpowers I didn't even know I had.

"And so for me, understanding that I never felt good enough, which makes me feel like I need to continually prove myself, means that I can be the most amazing champion for others who feel the same way. This is my superpower, and it reveals itself as a tremendous amount of empathy, an infectious amount of confidence, and the ability to give those I work with hope.

You see, as a digital marketing agency, PHANTA is a service-based business. And like most service-based businesses I spent years thinking that we were our customer's heroes. They would come to us when they were facing what seemed an impossible challenge, and we would ride in to save the day. But I realized that we're not the heroes—our customers are the heroes of their own journey. We're simply the guide. We're not Luke; we're Obi-Wan.

Pairing up that newfound understanding with my super-powers—empathy, confidence, and hope—means that I can connect with others on a deeper level. It gets real, it forces me to challenge myself, my team, and the customer, because we're not in this to simply produce a video or build a lead generation campaign—we're in this to show all those who doubt us how wrong they are.

And so, when I first meet with an entrepreneur, I want to know that they're looking to build something extraordinary. I listen to see if they have something to prove. I question if they're going to give up when it gets hard. I scrutinize everything that they're saying to ensure they're going to make the investment of time, money, and emotional commitment it takes to build something that matters."

And if I feel they have it, I stop, take a breath, and lean in to tell them this:

"I can't tell you what's going to work, or not work—at least not yet—but I can tell you where we will be exactly one year from now. One year from now you will be sitting in that chair, and I will be sitting right here across from you and here's what will have happened...

And then I proceed to paint the picture for exactly what could happen. The wins we may see and the setbacks we may face. The ups and the downs we'll face together. And all of the unknowns we'll have attacked and have learned how to overcome.

I paint the picture of one year from now because I know what's possible in a year. I understand what focus, resources, and an emotional commitment to making it happen can achieve. I can say with total confidence that things will go wrong, but what's the alternative? The work has to be done—by us, by our clients, or by someone else, but it has to be done.

And so my team and I will be there for the customer, to guide them through the whole process. I make a promise to the client that if they don't give up, together we'll prove their doubters wrong. I tell them one year from now we'll raise a glass to the year we've had and say, 'Look at what we've done.' I know they have something to prove, they just need someone to have their back."

That's Mark and his story. It's time to tell yours.

The man with something to prove: Mark Drager. He's been a friend for over a decade and inspired the first "Top 10 Rules for Success" video I ever did. He also filmed my first-ever YouTube video on Walt Disney.

TELL YOUR STORY

"It's important that we share our experiences with other people. Your story will heal you and your story will heal somebody else. When you tell your story, you free yourself and give other people permission to acknowledge their own story."

—IYANLA VANZANT

Now we get to see how much of a leader you are.

It's time to share your *Why*. Your story is needed to heal others. But here's what happens when most people find their *Why* and start telling their story: they summarize. They give a high-level, broad overview of what happened. I don't just need to know you went through the same thing I'm going through. I need to know you *felt* the same way I *feel*.

Remember to connect with people emotionally first.

A summary of what happened to you is too logical. And logic alone won't make people change. If I told you that I struggled as an entrepreneur and was making $300 per month, but then I eventually made it out by grinding away, and you can do the same, that's the truth, but it's a safe summary that doesn't mean anything. It doesn't connect with you.

Now what if I told you...

Becoming an entrepreneur was the scariest decision of my life. I had the opportunity to take my dream job, making six figures and traveling around the world, but I turned it down to make $300 per month and own 30 percent of a startup. I feared I was making the worst decision of my life and throwing my education away. I ate the same bean salad for lunch every day because it filled me up and was all I could afford. When we got a new client, we went to McDonald's to celebrate and shared a large fries because we couldn't afford the whole meal. I told my friends I couldn't go out with them because I was "hustling" and "living the entrepreneur life," but the reality was I couldn't afford the twenty dollars for pizza and beer. I felt isolated, alone, worthless, and that I was a loser. Why was I such a loser? Because I was working all day, every day, and getting no results. And then one day I told my partner, "I quit." I couldn't handle it. I was tired of being broke. I was tired of being embarrassed. I was tired of trying to impress people. I was tired of being ashamed. I was tired. I needed to feel like I had some kind of value again. I hit rock bottom. And then I discovered the secret that would not just transform my business but also change my whole life. The secret that got me sales, put real money in my bank account, exploded my customer base, and within two years led to my company being acquired and me not having to worry about money again... Do you want to know my secret? Do you feel more connected to me now? Do you see the difference between logical summaries and telling your story with feelings and emotions?

Here's how you can tell your story.

HOW TO TELL A GREAT STORY

"Every great story seems to begin with a snake."

—NICOLAS CAGE

There are three crucial elements to a great story: struggle, transformation, mission

You start with the struggle. What did you go through? What's the story behind your *Who* and your *Why*? Why was it so painful? I need to feel your pain. This isn't just any pain; this is the most painful moment of your life. Make me *feel* it with you. That's the only way I can compare my struggle to yours and feel like you get me because you're just like me. Maybe you need to change the names, genders, or roles of the people involved in your story. The characters can change so you don't throw a real person under the bus, but the feeling remains. That's what's most important. You need to get emotional when writing about your struggle. That's how you know it's working. If you don't feel it, others won't either. And if they don't feel you, they won't listen to you.

Next, talk about your transformation.

You did something to get through the pain. You stood up to someone. You changed your environment. You believed in yourself. Michael Edwards didn't listen to the doctors and healed himself with meditation. Mark Drager used faith to get him through handling an abusive, alcoholic stepfather who made him feel worthless. What did you do? How did you transform? How did you go from a caterpillar to a butterfly? This part of your story gives people hope that it's possible to overcome. That life doesn't have to suck forever. That we don't need to live in the shadows, in fear, in despair, in depression. There is a better life out there for us. Your transformation means I can transform as well.

You end with your mission.

Now that you've shown what you struggled through and how you transformed, you're on a mission to help others. That's your *Why*. You're here to help. You want to lift as many people as you can out of what you went through. And because I understand your struggle, and I see your transformation, I believe in your mission too.

Those are the three sections of a great story. Make them powerful.

Each section should make you emotional. Writing about your struggle should make you angry or want to cry. Writing about your transformation should make you feel hopeful and empowered. Writing about your mission should make you feel bold and inspired. Again, if you don't feel it, neither will the people reading it.

"But I'm not strong enough to do this. I'm not an inspiring leader."

3 KEY ELEMENTS OF A STORY

**THE CRUCIAL ELEMENTS TO A GREAT STORY ARE:
STRUGGLE, TRANSFORMATION, MISSION**

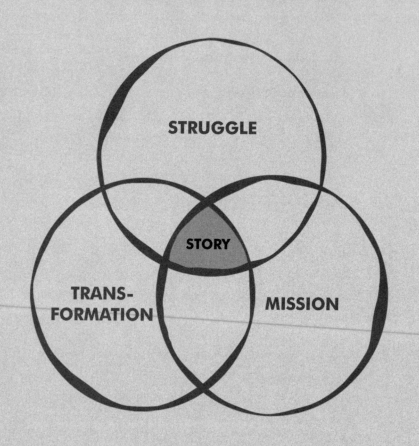

"Storytelling is the most powerful way to put ideas into the world." - Robert McKee

I AM NOT ENOUGH

"You alone are enough.
You have nothing to prove to anybody."

—MAYA ANGELOU

Who are you to be a leader helping other people transform?

You didn't go to school for this. You're not the biggest expert in the world. You don't have the resources other people have. You don't have the skills other people have. You don't even know what you're doing...and now you're on a mission? That's ridiculous. All of those things may be true. But it doesn't mean you can't help. Here's what you need to remember:

You can help the person you were five years ago.

The person you are today can help the person you were five years ago. You know more, have more confidence, have more experience, and can give specific guidance to the person you were five years ago. So you must. Because there are so many people who are like the old you. And those people need you.

Look at my story.

There are lots of entrepreneurs who have had more success than I have. There are many personal-development gurus that have more knowledge than I have. So should I not try? Should I not create videos? Should I not write books? Should I not do workshops, seminars, and speeches? At the time of this writing, over a quarter of a billion people have watched my videos and learned from them. I get comments every day from people who say how important what I do is to them—people like the woman who said she got in her car with the intention of driving off a bridge and killing herself, but on the drive she put one of my videos on in the car. The video inspired her, so she turned around, went home, and chose life. People like the man who said growing up his parents always told him that black people were n******, but because I profiled a black man on my channel, he was willing to put his prejudice aside for five minutes to give the video a chance. He then let me know his story and thanked me for giving him a new perspective, because he learned from a black man. I didn't set out to try to save lives or solve racism. I'm just trying to help entrepreneurs. But in the process of doing this work, countless positive ripple effects come out. When you give people hope and a path, amazing things will happen. There are so many comments from people who have consumed my content and had their lives changed. What if I had never created anything because I felt I wasn't good enough, because I wasn't enough of an expert, because I wasn't someone like Tony Robbins? So many people would not have been helped because of my insecurities and unwillingness to step up. I don't need to be Tony Robbins to help. You don't need to be Tony either.

Even Tony Robbins isn't Tony Robbins.

TONY ROBBINS
ISN'T TONY ROBBINS

"If you do what you've always done, you'll get what
you've always gotten."

—TONY ROBBINS

I see Tony Robbins as a hero in the personal-development space.

He's at the top. He's done the work. He's had decades of experience. He's absolutely obsessed with getting people to grow. He's the best there is. So a couple of years ago I wanted to see him in action and took four people from my team to go to one of his events, *Unleash the Power Within*, in California.

It was amazing, but on the first day something unexpected happened.

Tony's team suggests that if you come with people you know, you sit apart from each other. The intention is for you to have your own experience and express yourself without being worried about what the people you came with will think of you.

So I was sitting next to a couple who were also there for the first time.

Tony's events aren't just a brain dump of knowledge. He has you moving. You're dancing, hugging, and high fiving the people around you. You share with your neighbors and get to know why they came and what they're hoping to learn. I connected with the couple next to me and noticed that while their energy was high at the start of the day, by the afternoon the husband started tuning out. The wife was still jumping and involved, but the husband stopped standing up and jumping and stayed in his seat. He listened, but passively. The wife was trying to get him to stand up and get involved, but he ignored her. Eventually she stopped trying. We all jumped. He sat down.

Then the unthinkable happened.

Tony had just finished giving us a new set of tools and wanted us to celebrate. So the lights went down, the music went up, and it was a party. As I was standing up and dancing, the husband, who was sitting down, fell asleep. Tony was yelling. Music was blasting. The stadium was shaking. And this guy was passed out in his chair. I couldn't believe it. I was also jealous that someone could sleep through all that noise, since I'm such a light sleeper. His wife angrily woke him up once she saw him. He grumbled a bit, struggled to stay awake for the next hour, and then got up, left his seat, and never came back. The wife stayed and kept doing the exercises and activities, but half an hour later she started sitting down and was losing energy. I tried to do the activities with her and support her, but it was obvious that her mind was now on her husband and no longer on the event. At the next break she left too and never came back.

Tony Robbins, the best of the best, had a man pay thousands of dollars for a ticket only to fall asleep and walk out on the first day.

*I took my wife and team to see Tony at his **Unleash the Power Within** event in Los Angeles. It was my first time seeing Tony, and we sat in general admission.*

Tony invited me back the next year, so I went with my friend Mark Drager. We had better seats and got to hang with Tony backstage for a little bit this time.

YOU'RE NEVER DONE GROWING

"The only limit to your impact is
your imagination and commitment."

—TONY ROBBINS

The point of that story isn't to attack Tony Robbins.

I love Tony. I've learned so much from him over the years. I had a great time at that event, as did my team. I thought the event was life changing. But the experience with that couple showed me that even Tony Robbins isn't perfect. He's still growing. And if Tony Robbins loses some people and makes mistakes, it's okay if I do too!

Tony is crazy about constantly growing.

He's been doing events for decades. But after each show, even though he and his team are tired, they'll get together, celebrate the work they did, and then immediately get right to asking themselves, "How can we make it better next time? What did we miss this time that we must improve on?" He's obsessed with getting feedback and constantly growing. That's why he's the best. It wouldn't surprise me if someone on his team found the couple I was sitting next to and interviewed them about the experience so they could make their next event better, even if that means they'd lose just one less couple from the session.

You will never know everything.

There will always be something new to learn. There will always be more experiences, more knowledge, more tools, more resources. Forever. Perfect does not exist. If you wait until you know everything before you start helping, you'll never start. You'll be ninety-five years old, still waiting for the perfect time, and then it'll be too late.

It's time to embrace the *AND*.

You aren't the biggest expert *AND* you can help people. You can teach what you know *AND* you can keep learning. You will never be ready *AND* you must start now. Being a perfectionist has already killed too many of your dreams. You need to stop it right now. You're never done growing. Now start helping today, because the world needs you.

(When my mom read this page she said it reminded her of the famous Chinese proverb, "The best time to plant a tree was twenty years ago. The second best time is now.")

*That's your **Why** and how you can use it to empower others! Did you catch all of it? Here are the quick highlights.*

SECTION HIGHLIGHTS: YOUR *WHY*

"I learned that courage was not the absence of fear, but the triumph over it. The brave man is not he who does not feel afraid, but he who conquers that fear."

—NELSON MANDELA

Your *Why* Highlights

- Your *Why* is your purpose, and your purpose comes from your pain.
- Your purpose is to help other people who are currently facing the same struggle you went through.
- Whatever you went through that made you feel worthless is the seed of your purpose. Helping others who are currently facing those same challenges will fill you up.
- You can't do anything great without having had some great pain.
- You want to live a service life instead of a surface life.
- If you're not happy, it's because you're not serving.
- The help that will resonate most with you comes from your pain, your story.

- Comfort is the enemy of greatness.
- When you find your purpose, it gives you the strength to do things that you never thought were possible. It gives you new courage because you're on a mission.
- *"We have the tendency to run away from suffering and to look for happiness. But, in fact, if you have not suffered, you have no chance to experience real happiness."* (Thich Nhat Hanh)
- You were not meant to photocopy your day over and over again.
- If you suffer from compassion fatigue, then you need to figure out what balance looks like for you and create a schedule that supports it.
- You need to connect with people emotionally before logically.
- Your silence perpetuates everyone's silence.
- There are three crucial elements to a great story: struggle, transformation, mission.
- If you don't feel your story, neither will the people reading or hearing it.
- When you give people hope and a path out of pain, amazing things will happen.
- If Tony Robbins loses some people and makes mistakes, it's okay if you do too!
- Perfect does not exist. If you wait until you know everything before you start helping, you'll never start.

STEP 3

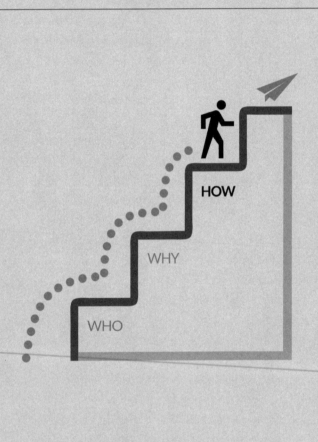

HOW

WHY

WHO

YOUR HOW

YOUR *HOW* = YOUR PASSION

"Passion is energy. Feel the power that comes from
focusing on what excites you."

—OPRAH WINFREY

My *Who* is #Believe

It's my most important core value, as discussed in the first part
of this book. But I can #Believe in anyone. Give me any human
facing any set of circumstances, and I'll #Believe in them. I'll
encourage them. I'll support them. I can't help it. Finding your
Who gives you some clarity, but it's not enough. It's only a
piece of the puzzle to find fulfillment. You need your *Why* and
your *How*.

My *Why* is helping entrepreneurs.

My biggest pain was struggling being an entrepreneur—not just
struggling to make money, but also struggling with self-doubt,
insecurities, fear, and anxiety. I think being an entrepreneur
is one of the hardest things you'll ever do in your life. And it's
especially hard when you go on your journey alone, without
guidance, help, or someone to #Believe in you. So my *Why* is to
help entrepreneurs not struggle as much as I did.

The last step is to find your *How.*

There are many ways I could #Believe in entrepreneurs. If you were growing your business and needed to move to a new office, I could help you move. I'd love the fact that you were expanding, and the end result would be me #Believing in you. But there's a problem: I don't enjoy packing boxes or moving.

You need to enjoy the *process,* not just the *end result.*

This is where so many people fall down. They say they'll do *whatever it takes* to win, but the reality is, they won't. Successful people love the process. They love the game. They love doing it. Jerry Seinfeld calls it the "torture you can endure." If you stepped into my schedule, it should be torture for you. Same thing if I stepped into yours. If you're doing it right, it should be torture for someone else. But for you, it's amazing. Now, you may not enjoy every moment of every day, but overall you're doing work that you love. When you can combine your core value (*Who*), with your purpose (*Why*), with doing work that you love (*How*), it's a home run. We already have identified your *Who* and *Why.* Now let's find your *How.*

Let's start by learning from one of the most successful women of all time.

THE MARY KAY ASH SUCCESS STORY

"So many women just don't know how great they really are. They come to us all vogue outside and vague on the inside."

—MARY KAY ASH

Mary Kay Ash changed the game for women entrepreneurs.

And just like every successful person, her success was rooted in her pain. While her husband was off fighting during WWII, she needed a way to support herself, so she joined Stanley Home Products to sell household and cleaning products. When her husband returned from the war, he ran off with another woman, leaving Mary Kay with three children to support on her own. She made Stanley Home Products her full-time career and quickly had success, eventually being named the "Queen of Sales" for being the company's most successful saleswoman.

But Stanley held her back.

Mary Kay wanted a promotion but she kept being passed over. She was a top producer, but men with less talent and knowledge were promoted ahead of her. She spent over a decade with Stanley, watching them continue to hold her back until she finally decided enough was enough. She left Stanley for a competitor, World's Gift.

Unfortunately, not much changed.

She spent the next decade at World's Gift extending their distribution into forty-three states and earning a seat on their board of directors. But every suggestion she gave the board for how to expand was met with immediate rejection. She was told, "Oh, Mary Kay, you're thinking just like a woman." In 1962, she was training a man who was then promoted to be her supervisor and was given twice her salary. Enraged, Mary Kay quit the company to take early retirement.

Mary Kay's story is one of limitation and lack of appreciation.

Her husband ran off with another woman. She was the top saleswoman at her first job but they didn't promote her. She expanded her second company but had to see her trainee become her boss at double her income. She faced limitations, neglect, and a lack of appreciation. Two of her most famous quotes are:

1. "Don't limit yourself. Many people limit themselves to what they think they can do. You can go as far as your mind lets you. What you believe, remember, you can achieve."
2. "Everyone wants to be appreciated, so if you appreciate someone, don't keep it a secret."

Now you understand her **Why.** *It was time to turn that pain into a purposeful* **How.**

MARY KAY'S HOW

"People fall forward to success."

—MARY KAY ASH

Mary Kay Ash decided to write a guide.

She wanted to help other women who were struggling to find their way in the corporate world. She hoped that by writing this guide, she could help other women avoid some of the same pitfalls that she fell into. Her pain of being passed over as a woman in the business world became her purpose of helping other women in the same position.

She made two lists.

The first list detailed all of her negative experiences—what happened, how to recognize it, and strategies to avoid it. The second list was what she thought an ideal business, a dream company, should do for working women with families. On that list were three core ideas: 1. Treat everyone equally. 2. Base promotions on merit. 3. Choose products based on their sales performance and marketability, rather than profitability.

In looking over that second list, she had a "Eureka" moment.

She thought, "Why am I theorizing about a dream company? Why don't I just start one?" And that's exactly what she did. Her first product was a skin softener from a local entrepreneur who she had been buying from for ten years. With her life savings, she bought the recipe for the skin softener, got a small store-front in Dallas, and hired a local manufacturer to create her new product. She went all in. She handled sales and marketing while her second husband dealt with financial and legal issues.

Then disaster struck.

Her second husband, and business partner, had a heart attack one month before their launch and died. Ash's lawyer and accountant were convinced that she wouldn't succeed without her husband's help, and they tried to dissuade her from starting. She had seen this story way too often and wasn't going to let it hold her back. Mary Kay Cosmetics opened its doors September 13, 1963. By the end of her first year, she had $198,000 in sales. After her second year, she had $800,000 and over 3,000 women selling for her. She would constantly tell the women who worked for her, "I created this company for you." Today, Mary Kay Ash is a billionaire and has over 3.5 million salespeople worldwide. She turned decades of neglect and being passed over into a force for women around the world.

If Mary Kay Ash could find a different way to stand, so could I.

MARY KAY ASH'S 3 IDEAS

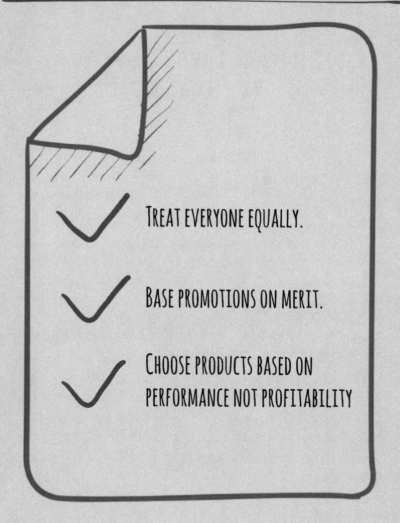

✓ TREAT EVERYONE EQUALLY.

✓ BASE PROMOTIONS ON MERIT.

✓ CHOOSE PRODUCTS BASED ON PERFORMANCE NOT PROFITABILITY

"When you come to a roadblock, take a detour."
- Mary Kay Ash

FINDING A DIFFERENT WAY TO STAND

"The only way to endure the quake is to adjust your stance. You can't avoid the daily tremors.
They come with being alive. These experiences are really gifts that force us to step to the right or left in search of a new center of gravity. Don't fight them.
Just find a different way to stand."

—OPRAH WINFREY

Remember when I told you that the worst day of my life was quitting on my business?

Well, I woke up the next day and decided that I couldn't quit. I told myself that I would rather know and fail than not know. But I knew that I couldn't keep going the way I was, because I was putting in a crazy number of hours and trying an insane amount of things, but nothing was working. I had to do something differently.

That's when it hit me.

I wasn't the first person to sell software. Someone had figured it out already. What if I just modeled what worked for them and applied it to my business? I thought about the biggest software entrepreneur: Microsoft founder Bill Gates. I researched his story to know how he got started. I didn't care how he makes an extra million dollars now; I wanted to know how he got his *first* million. Maybe if I understood that, I could learn from it and get my business off the ground.

Bill Gates saved my business.

I haven't met Bill Gates yet, but when I do, I want to shake his hand and thank him for saving my company. Gates built Microsoft through partnerships. He found other people who were selling to his target audience and looked for a way to work together. I had nothing to lose, so I applied the strategy to my business. Within a few months, I had my first deal for $13,500. That may not seem like a lot of money to you, but for me, it was like I had won the lottery. I was only making $300 per month, so $13,500 was a lifesaver. And, more importantly, it gave me hope that I could be a successful entrepreneur.

I learned I could get success by modeling success.

And then I applied it to everything. Don't know the answer to something? Model success! Someone has figured it out before. You don't need to be a genius and come up with every idea yourself. Just see who has won already and model their success. It won't take you all the way to the finish line, but it can take you 80 percent of the way, which makes everything a lot easier.

I found a path that would save my business. I'd later realize that I also found a path that would impact millions of entrepreneurs.

THE EVAN CARMICHAEL PATH

"I wanted to help entrepreneurs not feel the same pain I suffered, and the way I'd do it is by teaching what saved me: modeling success."

—EVAN CARMICHAEL

After applying the modeling-success strategy, my company started taking off.

We got more customers, partnerships, and exposure and eventually got acquired. It was a crazy three years where I went from having zero money and eating beans for lunch every day to having more money than I'd ever seen in my life. I wasn't forced to leave my company like Mary Kay Ash was, but I still woke up the day after I sold my business having no idea what to do next. My company was a huge chunk of my life. And now it was gone. What would I do next?

I wanted to help entrepreneurs.

I didn't know about *Who*, *Why*, *How*, or that purpose comes from pain. If I had, it would have shortcut my path. But I did know that I wanted to help entrepreneurs not feel the same pain I suffered, and the way I'd do it is by teaching what saved me: modeling success.

So I launched a website.

At the time, I was being asked to speak in places like Mexico and Brunei to tell my young-entrepreneur success story. I created a website to share where I was speaking and how people could find me. But I also wanted to tell the stories of other famous entrepreneurs. I figured if learning from Bill Gates could save my business, then it might help other struggling business owners save their companies too.

I profiled my heroes.

I told Bill Gates's story, but then quickly expanded to include other legends like Mary Kay Ash, Steve Jobs, Oprah Winfrey, and Howard Hughes. At the start I wasn't making money. I just knew I had to do it. I knew it was important for the few people who were checking out my website. I knew I had to find a way to keep doing it because it filled my soul. This was potentially life-changing information, if I could get people to read it. It was also fun to create and put together. With daily consistency, I eventually built a team of eight people and created 100,000 pages of content that received millions of views.

Then I shut it all down and moved to YouTube because I stopped enjoying the process.

MY YOUTUBE EXPERIMENT

"I liked the process of making videos.
I wasn't very good at it, but I liked it."

—EVAN CARMICHAEL

I got into YouTube as a test.

I love small tests. I love experimenting with ideas. I love seeing how new things work. You never know how it's going to work out, and the best way to know is to try. You can't think your way through liking sushi. You need to try tasting it. I released my first YouTube video on April 14, 2009. In it, I told the story of Walt Disney and what entrepreneurs can learn from his success. At the time I had a successful website and a team of people working for me to help me grow it.

But I wasn't enjoying the process.

The end result of over 100,000 pages of content on my website was that entrepreneurs were being helped. I loved that. #Believing in entrepreneurs is my *Who* and *Why*. But there was a problem. I didn't like being a website-content factory. I liked the end result, but not the process. And I had studied enough successful people to know that you will never be the best at something when you don't love the process of doing it. So I experimented.

YouTube was the experiment that stuck.

I wasn't very good at making videos. My first video was awkward. In it, I'm sitting down with a blue suit and red tie. I'm trying to memorize my lines. I'm sweating and stressed. I'm introverted and extremely uncomfortable speaking to the camera. But you know what? I liked it. My friend helped me film it and asked me if I was going to be a "one-take wonder," meaning I would film the whole video perfectly in one take. Wow, was that far from the truth. I did it over, and over, and over again. Eventually I managed to get the words out without stumbling or forgetting. It's an embarrassing video to look back on, but I've kept it up on my YouTube channel all these years because it shows my journey.

I liked the process of making videos.

I'm a visual learner, and I enjoyed making something visual. I had no natural talent for it and had so many issues and insecurities to overcome, but I liked the process. So I dedicated myself to getting better, and once I started making some money doing it, I shut down my website, turned off 100,000 pages of content, killed that entire revenue stream, and moved my eight team members over to help me work on my YouTube channel. Hundreds of millions of views later, the rest is history. Making videos is now my *How*.

You get success when you love the process.

Here's a screen capture from my first YouTube video. If you search for "Walt Disney Documentary—Disney's Success Story" on YouTube, you'll find it!

In the first year of the video being up, I only got three comments. Two of the three were from my mom and sister. Woo!

YOU HAVE TO ENJOY THE PROCESS

"The most difficult thing is the decision to act,
the rest is merely tenacity. The fears are paper tigers.
You can do anything you decide to do. You can act
to change and control your life; and the procedure,
the process is its own reward."

—AMELIA EARHART

Successful people enjoy the process.

I've studied more successful people than almost anyone, and
they all have different personalities, religions, skin colors, backgrounds, political viewpoints, etc. But the one thing they all
have in common is they love the process. They love the work.
The advice I see repeated most often is some variation of: love
what you do, be passionate, and do what excites you. Here are
some examples:

> "Your work is going to fill a large part of your life, and the
> only way to be truly satisfied is to do what you believe is great
> work. And the only way to do great work is to **love what you
> do**. If you haven't found it yet, keep looking. Don't settle."
>
> —Steve Jobs

145

*"Nothing is as important as passion. No matter what you want to do with your life, **be passionate**."*

—Jon Bon Jovi

*"Feel the power that comes from focusing on what **excites you**."*

—Oprah Winfrey

Successful people love the doing, not just the end result of what they're doing.

This is a very important distinction. If you know your *Who* and your *Why*, it's very easy to get locked into any number of paths that will give you an end result that you enjoy but a process you don't. That's why the *How* is so important to your success. The *Who* and the *Why* aren't complete without the right *How*.

There is no island.

Imagine that you're out in the ocean swimming. Most people live their life swimming, trying to get to the island. That island is retirement. That island is relaxation. That island seems like freedom. But successful people don't want to reach the island. They want to swim forever. Because swimming is the true freedom and there is no retirement from your purpose. You don't want there to be. It's ultimate bliss.

Loving the process just might lead you to buying an NFL franchise like Gary Vaynerchuk.

GARY VEE AND THE NEW YORK JETS

"I want to own the New York Jets, that's what I want. And I absolutely believe I am going to own the Jets."

—GARY VAYNERCHUK

Gary Vaynerchuk's life goal is to buy the New York Jets. But, as he writes, it's not about the actual goal of buying the team. It's about the process:

"I don't care whether or not I end up buying the New York Jets." (And no, this has nothing to do with their current standing this season.)

The truth is, I just love the climb. I love the sweat, the long hours, the uncertainties, and the grind. Nothing in life comes easy, and when we're dealing with something as huge as a lifetime goal, it's likely that things will change throughout that journey—but that's okay. It's part of the process. And that process is what I love so much.

I've said it a few times before—the day that I actually buy the Jets is going to make me incredibly upset, because the climb will be "over." That's what really worries me—because, then what? By creating such a heavy north star, I never have to reset my goals. I'm a very big "shoot for the moon/land in the stars" type of guy. Always having that north star has allowed me to be a much more honorable and legacy-driven entrepreneur because now I'm trying to reach this gigantic goal of mine and do so with grace and dignity.

This north star that I've set for myself is a mechanism I use for a lot of things. Not only do the Jets represent to me what it meant to become an American, but it's also the ultimate Kickstarter campaign. If I get to an age where I don't think I can buy the Jets on my own, I believe that the way I built this narrative will guilt people into helping me make that dream come true.

And so, the honest truth is that I don't really give a sh*t about whether or not I end up buying the Jets. (But now, since I've gotten that out there, everybody is going to really freak out when I actually do buy the team. I'm smart like that.) For me though, the real win is in the process, the journey. Whether implicit or explicit, we all have incredible goals for ourselves. Some of us will achieve them and others won't. And that's perfectly fine. ***The key takeaway in establishing these goals is how we handled ourselves and those around us during that process.*** What relationships did we create? What stories can we tell? Whose lives did we affect for the better? That's what matters. It's not about the glory of reaching a personal goal, it's about the glory of relishing the journey and sharing in that accomplishment with those that helped us get there."

It's now time for you to find your How.

HOW TO FIND YOUR PASSION

"Every great dream begins with a dreamer.
Always remember, you have within you the strength,
the patience, and the passion to reach for the stars
to change the world."

—HARRIET TUBMAN

There are two ways to find your *How*.

The first is the *Recipe for Success*. It's how you saved yourself. You were in a hole. You were facing a lot of pain. You found your way out. That wasn't an accident. A lot of people never get out. They're still experiencing that pain and reliving it day after day. Your way out isn't a one-off occurrence. It's a recipe. It's a model. It's a blueprint. And it can help other people. Your passion, your *How* will be teaching the recipe to others and helping them get out as well.

The second is to use the *Passion Process,* where you think about all the work that you enjoy the results *as well as* the process. Liking the end result isn't enough. You have to like the work. Successful people love the process of achieving success, not just hitting the wins. Having a fulfilled life means actually living and enjoying your life, not just bouncing between milestones.

Both methods have three key steps.

Take some time for yourself, clear your mind, answer the questions honestly, and you'll find your passion. You'll get your *How* and find the final piece to the *Who, Why, How* process.

First, how did you save yourself?

HOW DID YOU SAVE YOURSELF?

"It's really not looking for someone to be your
superhero but for us to save ourselves
and to really understand that."

—KAREN CIVIL

You're your own superhero.

You struggled. You suffered massive pain. You made it through. You might not be all the way out, but you're stronger than you were before. Nobody came and did it for you. You decided that it was important to change and then took the steps to improve your life. How did you do it? What process did you go through? What did you try? What worked? What failed? These are the beginnings of finding your *How*.

What worked for you will work for others.

The process you went through to lift yourself from the hole you were in may not have been the smoothest ride, but there are lessons that other people can learn from it. Remember, your purpose is to help other people who are currently going through the massive pain you went through. So the solution that you found to heal and grow will be helpful to those people that you are trying to serve. If it worked for you then it just might work for them. And the fact that you probably tried lots of different things, most of which didn't work, will give you the ability to shortcut someone's path through pain faster. You struggled a lot, but others don't have to. You have a recipe that can help them.

Figure out your recipe for success.

What was the habit, action, mentality, or resource that made the difference? If you met yourself ten years ago when you were still struggling with this thing, what would you tell yourself to do? Did you change your environment? Did you meditate? Did you take a class? Did you alter your morning routine? Did you adjust your mindset? What did you do, step by step?

Here are the three most important questions to ask:

1. When did you decide that something had to change?
2. What was the first thing that you did to start the change?
3. How did you sustain the momentum?

This is your *Recipe for Success*. It's your blueprint for how someone like you can break free of what you had to deal with. And there are many people who are in the same situation as you were and need to break free.

Let's apply this Recipe for Success with some real life examples.

YOUR RECIPE FOR SUCCESS

1 WHEN DID YOU DECIDE
SOMETHING **HAD TO CHANGE?**

2 WHAT'S THE **FIRST THING** YOU
DID TO START THE CHANGE?

3 HOW DID YOU **SUSTAIN THE
MOMENTUM?**

APPLYING THE RECIPE FOR SUCCESS

"Long ago, I realized that success leaves clues, and that people who produce outstanding results do specific things to create those results."

—TONY ROBBINS

We'll start with Mary Kay Ash:

When did she decide something had to change?
The early signs were there from her first husband leaving her. Then her first company did not promote her after she was their best salesperson. Then her second company ignored her ideas because she was just "thinking like a woman." But she decided something had to change when her trainee was promoted to be her supervisor and was given twice her salary. That was *it*.

What was the first thing she did to start the change?
She wrote a guide for women to have success in the corporate world based on her own experience. Then she decided it was going to be the tool she would use to start her own business instead of just a guide for others.

How did she sustain the momentum?

She kept reminding herself, "What you believe, you can achieve." When her husband died a month before launching her first store, she kept going. When her accountant and lawyer told her to quit, she kept going. She reminded herself that she was capable, even though the outside world thought she would fail.

Here are my quick answers:

When did I decide something had to change?

The day after I told my business partner that I quit our business.

What was the first thing I did to start the change?

I modeled the success of Bill Gates and applied it to my business by forming marketing partnerships with companies.

How did I sustain the momentum?

Every time I didn't know how to do something, I'd ask myself, "Who has figured this out and how can I model their success?" Now it's your turn. Apply the three questions to yourself and discover the recipe for how you can help others.

Now we can drill further into your How with the Passion Process.

THE PASSION PROCESS

"There is no passion to be found playing small—
in settling for a life that is less than the one you are
capable of living."

—NELSON MANDELA

**The *Passion Process* will give you clarity on how you
can achieve your purpose.**

Step 1: Make a list of all the ways you've helped people.

List every time that you've helped somebody. Use the worksheets (see the start of this book to get yours for free) or take
out a piece of paper and fill it with the different ways you've
brought joy to others. Remember, humans are built to serve, so
your passion will come from contributing to making someone
else's life better. Here are some examples:

- Met with a stressed-out friend over coffee
- Left a testimonial for a company you hired
- Introduced two people who are now working together
- Spoke at an event to share your knowledge
- Bought a stranger a meal on the street

- Helped organize an event for a cause you believed in
- Found an article and sent it to a friend who could use it

There's no right or wrong. Just fill the page with the things you did where you enjoyed the end result. You helped someone and it made you feel good. Try to get at least twenty examples.

Step 2: Underline the activities that you enjoyed.

Not all activities are created equal. Look at the list you just made of all the ways you've helped people and underline the ones where you enjoyed the actual process, not just the result. Maybe you love that the two people you connected are now working together, but you didn't love the process of brainstorming who in your network could help each other or the process of introducing them. Maybe you enjoyed helping people by speaking at an event, but you didn't enjoy the process of speaking.

Step 3: Narrow it down to your top three.

These are the activities that you enjoyed the most. You loved the end result *and* you loved the process. This is where you truly come alive, and you need to figure out ways to do it more often. Just like I can help you move your office and will enjoy the result, which is me #Believing in a new entrepreneur, but since I don't love moving, I shouldn't open up a moving company.

This section is personal because I made it for my wife, Nina.

THE PASSION PROCESS

1. MAKE A LIST
of all ways you've
helped people.

2. UNDERLINE
the activities
you've enjoyed.

3. NARROW IT
down to your
top 3 choices.

"Stop chasing the money & start chasing the passion."
- Tony Hsieh

HELPING MY WIFE FIND CLARITY

"People are remarkably bad at remembering long lists
of goals... Clarity comes with simplicity."

—BRENDON BURCHARD

You can thank Nina for the entire *How* section.

She and I went on a road trip to Boston. I had just told her that I
was going to take her to every city in America with over a million
people, and Boston was going to be the first city. It was close by,
had over a million people, and Nina had never been to it. The
city was amazing, and we met a lot of mission-driven entrepreneurs who we helped grow.

The drive home was even more life changing.

There's something about an eight-hour drive that can get to
meaningful conversations—especially after you've just had an
amazing weekend helping people find their purpose and put
it to work. At the halfway point in our drive, the conversation
turned to Nina. She knew that her *Who* was #Care. She knew
that her *Why* was because when she came to Canada, members

in her family were picked on and made to feel less than. Great! She knew she wanted to care for people, and she knew where it came from.

"But...what am I supposed to do?"

At first I didn't even know how to react to that question. "What do you mean? You find ways to care for people who are picked on and made to feel less than." She replied, "Yes, but how?" In my mind, she just needed to start. *Just go*, I thought. *You'll figure it out.* What I came to understand was, she needed a process to follow—something with a little more structure than, "Just go figure it out." And that's where the *Passion Process* came from. I told her to do the three steps I just asked you to do on the previous page. She had never thought about it before. So, while I kept driving toward our hometown of Toronto, I told her to make a list of all the ways she has helped people. "Right now?" she asked. "Yep—right now," I replied. "We still have four hours until we get home. We have time. What else is happening in the next four hours that is more important?" She pulled out her phone and quietly got to work.

Then we took the next step.

Working on her phone, she underlined the instances where she enjoyed the process and the results. For example, she enjoyed helping me in my business by doing the accounting for my company, but she didn't enjoy the process of accounting. She just enjoyed the fact that she helped me. Awesome, but not enough. She needed to enjoy the process too.

Here are her answers.

Me and my wife, Nina, on our trip to Boston, where I came up with the **How** part of the **Who, Why, How** process. Here we are doing a tour of the famous baseball stadium, Fenway Park.

NINA'S PASSION PROCESS

"It makes me feel good, knowing that I have helped."

—NINA CARMICHAEL

This is what Nina wrote on the trip back to Toronto.

The underlined ones are the ones where she enjoyed both the result and the process.

1. Organize an event like Toronto Dance Salsa helper event—makes me happy when I know that people are having a good time.
2. Work—help come up with better reconciliation template so that there is more control.
3. Help the new person from work to understand the system why this is the process.
4. Show the people that I trained how I organize my email so that they don't miss important emails.
5. Helped my brother pick up my niece and nephew when they needed—love my family.
6. My brother—bought some lobsters from my brother.
7. Helped my friend (who I knew when I was a baby) over ten years ago to move to Canada.

8. Help Evan accounting—love to help the person that l love.

9. Mail out books and entrepreneur cards for Evan.

10. Helped my parents fix their backyard.

11. Reached out to my cousin who is in the lawn mowing business to come cut my parents front yard. I offered to pay.

12. Surprised my colleague with coffee in the morning because I know she needs one. She is a really nice person. I really enjoyed going to grab a coffee with her.

13. Brought food to some people at work.

14. Want to donate to charity if I can; it makes me feel good, knowing that I have helped.

15. Always feel like I need to step up when no one volunteers to help.

16. Always wanted to jump in to help if my friends, family need help. Want my friends and family to be happy.

17. Recommend people to clinics or habits that help me with my health because I want the best for them.

18. Share my experience with my friends; let them feel that they are not alone.

She looked at the list a few times and reflected on what those activities meant to her.

Then she made a life-changing decision.

NINA DECIDED TO QUIT HER JOB

"If I quit having fun, then it's time for me
to quit working."

—CHARLAINE HARRIS

Remember earlier when I said humans were built to serve?

If you're not happy, it's because you're not serving enough. Some people are built to serve the world and others are built to serve the twenty-five people closest to them. Well, I'm the serve-the-world kind of guy. That's what makes me happy. And Nina is the opposite. She's the serve-the-twenty-five-closest-people kind of woman. That's reflected in her *Passion Process* list. If you read it carefully, you'll see that most of what she loves doing is helping her family and close friends. That's amazing self-awareness, and if she's ever feeling low, she knows she just needs to #Care for her family or close friends to lift her spirits. However, most of what's on her list doesn't point to a career option or how she should be spending her time.

But there was one that popped off the list.

The very first answer was organizing events for the Toronto Dance Salsa helpers. Once a quarter, she would help coordinate an activity for our school volunteers where we'd do something fun like laser tag or escape rooms and then have some food at a local restaurant. Nina would figure out the details, contact the venues, and create a memorable experience for everyone who came. She loved it. When she was in university, she even thought about starting an event-organizing business with her friend. The problem with Toronto Dance Salsa was that organizing their events wasn't a full-time job. Nowhere close. We only do them four times a year, and they don't take long to organize. I looked at my Evan Carmichael business and, while I spoke at events around the world each year, I wasn't organizing that much myself.

Then we made a radical decision.

I made the goal to take Nina to every city in North America with over a million people. We had just crossed Boston off of our list. We had another forty or so cities to go to. Nina loved organizing and helping her family. What if we did a tour across America where I would speak, we could see the cities, and Nina would organize the whole thing? We could go from just doing one city to doing over half the remaining cities on our list. We started building momentum. We decided on ninety days and twenty-three cities. Nina would quit her job and put her planning hat on. She booked the venues where I would speak, reserved places for us to sleep, coordinated with the tour partners that I lined up, connected with the people who bought tickets to the show, created our plan for what to see in each city and what restaurants to eat at, and on the day of each event she helped set up the room, check people in, keep me on track, and pack up when it was all done.

It also led to another bold decision.

NINA BECAME MY CHIEF HEART OFFICER

"Too often we underestimate the power of a touch,
a smile, a kind word, a listening ear, an honest
compliment, or the smallest act of caring, all of which
have the potential to turn a life around."

—LEO BUSCAGLIA

Nina loves and cares about the people close to her.

Look at her list again. She loves helping her family, surprising her friends, sharing experiences, and making recommendations. That's what makes her come alive. Nina is still in touch with people that she went to kindergarten with in China. That blows my mind. She stays in touch with all her friends and is always the glue in each relationship.

Could that work in my business?

Right now I have twenty-four people on my team around the world. What if my team became Nina's friends? What if she cared as much about them as she did for her colleagues at other jobs? If she poured her love, energy, and compassion into them, how much would that help my company? We set out to find out and made her my Chief Heart Officer.

What does a Chief Heart Officer Do?

We started by making a private Facebook group for everyone on my team, which Nina runs. She welcomes new people in and every week posts something about someone to the group. Someone had a work anniversary? Post it to the group. Had a baby? Moved into a new house? Going on vacation? Their favorite soccer team won a tournament? Post it to the group. She tries to switch it up every week so everyone gets an opportunity to be recognized. Having a team that is spread out around the world makes it nice to have a place for everyone to connect and cheer each other on.

She'll also coordinate special projects for my team to connect us to them more closely. My two video editors are in Montenegro, so we went to visit them, and my three-person team from Serbia came down to join us as well. Nina planned it all. She helped one of my team members get a visa to come to Canada to join us for a week for my Thought Leadership Academy event. Christina is going to stay at my place while in Canada, and Nina is coordinating everything.

Finally, she follows everyone on social media. She checks in daily to see if they've posted anything; she sends them love, cheers them on, and stays in touch with them—just like she does with her friends from kindergarten in China. They're getting the #Care that only Nina can bring.

I need this role because she's the complete opposite of me.

I DON'T LIKE TO HANG OUT

"Many of my filmmaking colleagues complain that after
the film is over you don't talk to us. I can't explain it to
them. I don't have anything else to say. I love you.
I miss you. But I miss you through the work."

—SHAH RUKH KHAN

I don't keep in touch with anybody.

If we're not working on something together, I'm probably not
talking with you. I love you. We're just probably not in touch.
I don't like to hang out. I just don't feel a need for it. It feels
like work, while actual work feels like fun. I used to think I was
crazy until I did a video on the Indian superstar actor Shah Rukh
Khan. In one of the clips he said:

> I'm unsocial. I'm very odd with people. So what happens
> is I have replaced people with work in my life. When I'm
> working, there are people I can interact with because some-
> where there is a wall that I'm not interacting with them
> socially. I'm interacting with them through this common
> goal that is the work so I can discuss with her or discuss
> with him and we're friends for that moment. Many of my
> filmmaking colleagues complain that after the film is over

you don't talk to us. I can't explain it to them. I don't have anything else to say. I love you. I miss you. But I miss you through the work. I'm very fond of a lot of people. A lot of people I love like family and I can't pick up the phone and talk with them. I can't socialize with them. I can't sit and chat with them but when we are working, I can just be with them. I have replaced loneliness, depression, and people with work.

This might read as sad and depressing, but it was liberating for me. Crazy liberating. I've told the stories of so many people over the years, and I've never heard anyone say anything close to this. "I love you. I miss you. But I miss you through the work." I totally get him.

But that's a very weird-duck mentality.

That mentality works for me, and when I'm working with someone on my team, they feel loved. But afterward, when the project is done and they may not be working as closely with me, I won't keep in touch. Not until the next project, and then we're back in it together. One woman on my team was unhappy because she wanted to be friends and hang out socially. I had to explain to her that I don't do that with anyone. I only hang out with Nina. That's enough to fill my social needs. But I love you. I want you to win and will do more for you than anyone. If you need me, you can count on me. For some people though, that's not enough. They need frequent social connection. So Nina has become a shining star for my business.

In writing this page, I found a huge missing piece as well.

I OVERLOOKED
SOMETHING HUGE

"Nothing is more expensive than a missed opportunity."

—H. JACKSON BROWN JR.

I'm writing this as I'm driving to New York City.

I have a couple of meetings, and my doctors haven't cleared me to fly yet because my neck is still broken and healing. So, we're driving. I can't drive yet either because I can't turn my head enough to see the blind spots. Nina is driving and singing to music. It's an eight-hour trip there and then eight hours back tomorrow. I'm typing away next to her; she has no idea I'm writing about her. It's weird writing about someone when they're right next to you, especially after you're looking at their answers to the *Passion Process* exercise. I'm filled with love, compassion, and gratitude for her all at once.

I realized I overlooked an important ingredient.

Looking back, most of the items on her list were helping family and close friends. The event-planning one directly led to her quitting her job so she could plan our trip. But there's something

171

that I totally ignored that just hit me hard in the face reading it back today. Number fourteen: "Want to donate to charity if I can; it makes me feel good that I have helped."

I don't donate much money to charity.

If my friends ask me to sponsor their bike ride for a charity or special cause, I'm pretty much always in, but it's very reactionary. I have no budget set aside for charity work. I show love through acts of service, so the way I give back is through my time—by speaking at charity events; by always having a percentage of people get into my workshops or courses or events for free if they can't afford it; by donating my time to coach people who need help. Giving money just feels so clinical and sterile. But I value my time so much that if I'm giving it away in service, it really feels special to me.

And Nina's not involved in any of it.

She doesn't pick which organizations or entrepreneurs I give my time to. She *could*. We don't have a fund for special causes. We *could*. I realized just today in reviewing the *Passion Process* and her answers that I need to do a better job helping her here. It's something that she enjoys the results and the process of. It's a home run. And she spends zero time doing it. I'm going to talk with her tonight over dinner in New York to see what she wants to do. And that right there is the power of the *Passion Process*. If you know what makes you come alive, if you can find your *How* and then tie it to your *Who* and your *Why*, you're set. You're on the path to a purposeful, fulfilled life.

You need to keep your How relevant.

YOUR *HOW* CAN CHANGE

"You cannot change your destination overnight,
but you can change your direction overnight."

—JIM ROHN

I've got good news and...more good news for you.

Your *Who* is constant. It'll never change. Look at your *Who*.
Now imagine your life at ninety-five. You'll still care about
it. If anything, you'll care more. If you can't see yourself still
believing in it at ninety-five, you have the wrong *Who*. I'm going
to #Believe in people forever. Your *Why* is also constant. That
pain that you experienced will serve you for life. Helping people
who are currently going through the pain you experienced will
never get old. You'll never get tired of it. I'll love helping entrepreneurs forever. So that's good news. Just understanding those
two things means you know more about yourself and what you
need to do than most people on this planet.

Here's the other good news.

Unlike your *Who* and Why, your *How* isn't fully constant. On a
macro level it is. My way out of struggling as an entrepreneur was
modeling success, and so I teach people how to model success.
That will never get old. But on a micro level, it will change

173

frequently. Right now, I'm writing books and making YouTube videos. In the future, it'll be virtual-reality Evan and hologram Evan beaming into your living room. Every time a new platform comes up, every time a new technology disrupts, every time a new trend comes along, it's an opportunity for you to jump in and spread your message.

That change is what helps you win.

I make a lot of YouTube videos. Right now, the only person who I haven't been able to make a deal with is Jim Rohn. If you don't know Jim, he's one of the fathers of personal development. He's a legend. He was the mentor to Tony Robbins. But if you walk down the street and ask people if they know who Jim Rohn is, you'll get ninety-nine blank stares out of a hundred. That's the problem. This man is a genius! A pioneer! And nobody knows about him. Why? Because he's not relevant on the platforms that matter. Right now, YouTube matters. Instagram matters. Jim's team doesn't want to work with me because they want to sell DVDs, CDs, and VHS tapes of his material. Nobody's buying that. Who even still uses a DVD player, let alone a CD or VHS player? That's the problem—and it's why he has legend-level talent, but nobody knows him anymore. He's not relevant where it matters. If you stay current, you can gain attention with less experience. People are taking hacked versions of Jim's ideas, strategies, and plans, pushing them as their own, and displacing him. The decisions of Jim's team show that your *How* has to evolve. It has to change, or your message won't reach people.

That's your How, the last piece in the Who, Why, How formula. Did you catch all of it? Here are the quick highlights.

SECTION HIGHLIGHTS: YOUR *HOW*

"I've learned that people will forget what you said,
people will forget what you did, but people will never
forget how you made them feel."

—MAYA ANGELOU

Your *How* Highlights

- Your How is your passion; you need to enjoy the process, not just the end result.
- When you combine your core value (Who), with your purpose (Why), with doing work that you love (How), it's a home run.
- You may not enjoy every moment of every day, but overall you will be doing work that you love.
- "Everyone wants to be appreciated, so if you appreciate someone, don't keep it a secret." —Mary Kay Ash
- Just see who has won already and model their success.
- "The only way to endure the quake is to adjust your stance. You can't avoid the daily tremors. They come with being alive. These experiences are really gifts that force

us to step to the right or left in search of a new center of gravity. Don't fight them. Just find a different way to stand." (Oprah Winfrey)

- Find other people who are currently selling to your target audience and look for a way to work together.
- Don't know the answer to something? Model success!
- I shut down my website and moved to YouTube because I stopped enjoying the process.
- Successful people love the doing, not just the end result of what they're doing.
- Successful people don't want to reach the island. They want to swim forever.
- I'm trying to reach this gigantic goal of mine and do so with grace and dignity.
- The key takeaway to establish these goals is how we handled ourselves and those around us during the process.
- Having a fulfilled life means actually living and enjoying your life, not just bouncing from milestone to milestone.
- You're your own superhero.
- Remember, your purpose is to help other people who are currently going through the massive pain you went through. So the solution that you found to heal and grow will be helpful to those people you are trying to serve.
- What was the habit, action, mentality, or resource that made the difference?
- The Passion Process will give you clarity on how you can achieve your purpose.
- "Too often we underestimate the power of a touch, a smile, a kind word, a listening ear, an honest compliment, or the smallest act of caring, all *of which have the potential to run a life around.*" (Leo Buscaglia)

FROM PURPOSE TO PROFIT

"Profit isn't a purpose, it's a result. To have purpose means the things we do are of real value to others."
- Simon Sinek

YOU NEED TO MAKE MONEY

"If you work just for money, you'll never make it, but if you love what you're doing and you always put the customer first, success will be yours."

—RAY KROC

Money is important.

Some people think money is the most important thing. It's not. You might make money and then discover you still don't have any fulfillment and are not happy. Other people think money isn't important at all. They're wrong too. Money is amazing. Having it helps you do great things. Even if you're a charity, you need to figure out how to make money. If you don't make money, you can't do great things. It's not the number one priority, and it's not number one hundred, but it has to be in your top five.

This section is about making money from your purpose. You have to embrace that.

If you never learn how to make money from your purpose, you'll always end up needing a day job, and your purpose will become a hobby. If that sounds like a great life to you then I'm happy for you. If not, then you need to figure out a money-making model that makes sense—one that's consistent, one that's significant, one that can pay you so you can quit your job and succeed to the point where you are providing jobs for others and helping even more people. You can always give back. Whether you're giving a percentage of your profits to a cause or donating your time to the community, you can build in a plan to give things away for free. But if everything is free, the amount you can give will always be limited. If, however, you build a successful company that helps people and brings in money, the amount you can give back for free dramatically rises because you have a team, because you have profits, because you have an audience. So how do you make money?

Making money is about giving value.

Want to make a lot of money? Provide a lot of value. Want to make money quickly? Provide value quickly. How do you provide value? You solve a pain point. Well, good news! We just went through the process of finding a huge pain point of yours and understanding how you can solve it for others. That's what you sell. Some people who have that pain will pay you big money to help them solve it. Others can't afford to pay you at all. Make money from those who *can* pay so you build your business, support your lifestyle, build your dream, and give back to those who *can't* pay. That's what this section is about—having a big impact and making money while doing it, ethically, honestly, and in service of your mission.

Let's begin with how you get started with no money.

START WITH NO MONEY

"Rule number one: Never lose money.
Rule number two: Never forget rule number one."

—WARREN BUFFETT

Don't spend money until you're making money.

This is where so many entrepreneurs fail. You spend money you don't have. You want to start a t-shirt business, but to get the price breaks in production you need to order 5,000 shirts. So you drain your bank account, fill up your credit card, or borrow money from family to get started. Then you sell three shirts and have 4,997 sitting in your mom's garage.

Anybody can spend money. If I gave you a million dollars, you could find a million different ways to spend it. But you don't want to be in the spending money business. You want to be in the making money business!

But don't you need to spend money to make money?

Nope. To be clear, if you spend money, it will accelerate things. If those 5,000 t-shirts are in hot demand, the money you spent was well placed, and now you can grow even faster. The problem is, the first product rarely works out, and I don't want you to start

180

off being further in debt. So at the start, you *don't spend money*. You invest your *heart*, your *hustle*, your *energy*, your *passion*. But not your *money*. Don't spend your money until you're making money.

There is always a way to start smaller.

In fact, starting smaller will actually help you. Entrepreneurs are dreamers. We love imagining the type of company we can build and all the people we can help. But the bigger your dream, the more money you need, and because you don't have that kind of money, you don't do anything. Starting too big keeps your idea a dream that never comes to life.

Here's the secret: dream big; act small.

It's important to dream big. Your big dream will motivate you. It'll inspire you to keep going when things get tough. It'll be a rallying call for partners, suppliers, customers, and future employees. Keep a hold of your huge dream. And then act small. Find the smallest possible way to get started, to take the first step, to get some momentum going. Dream big; act small.

Let's take that t-shirt business model and make it work.

SELLING T-SHIRTS WITH NO MONEY

"Never spend money before you have earned it."

—THOMAS JEFFERSON

Don't order 5,000 t-shirts with money you don't have.

Here is a better way to do it, investing just your time, energy, and hustle. You start with the design. Are you going to design it, or do you need to get a designer? If it's you, awesome. Get to work. Finish your design. What are you waiting for? If you need help, then that's your next step. Don't pay for the design, though. Find people who will do it for no money. Maybe they're friends who just want to help. Maybe they're talented artists in your community who believe in your *Why* because you shared your story with them. Maybe it's someone who will come in on a joint venture for the first shirt, where you split the profits. There are lots of ways to do it. Don't spend money. Entrepreneurship is always about *resourcefulness* more than *resources*.

Next, find an on-demand printing service.

There are many options. Look them up online. You upload your design, pick the style and color of t-shirt you want to sell, set your price, and they give you a customized website link you can send people to. They will take care of printing, shipping, and returns. Now, they're going to take most of the profits because they are doing most of the work. And it's up to you to start marketing and let people know that it exists.

But why not keep all the profits and do it all myself?

This is the trap so many people fall into. It's true that if you sold all 5,000 shirts yourself, you'd likely make way more money. But if you sell only three, you're eating a big loss. You're giving up profit margin for risk. If you only sell three t-shirts using print-on-demand, you're not losing anything but your time. And now you can test lots of different designs. Maybe your first fourteen designs don't sell, but number fifteen finally pops! If you do it all yourself, you're broke after your first design and print run. When you keep your costs at zero, it lets you keep testing until you find a winner. Dream big; act small.

When you find a winner, expand!

Once you know you've got a winning design, take the money you've made from it and make an order. You know you can sell those shirts, and this time at a much higher margin. Once you start making money, you pour it back into the business to grow even faster. Money is like gasoline. Spray it on dead wood and it just gets soaked up. Spray it on a twig that has even a tiny flame and it'll ignite. Don't spray gas until you've got that flame.

Let me show you how I did it on my YouTube channel.

HOW I STARTED
WITH NO MONEY

"I had to follow my own advice: you invest your heart,
your hustle, your energy, your passion,
but not your money."

—EVAN CARMICHAEL

When I started my YouTube career I had money.

I had sold my first business and had money in my account. I had built a new business that was making money, and I had eight people on my team. Then I decided I wanted to try YouTube to see if I could reach more entrepreneurs to help them #Believe in themselves. But I had to follow my own advice: you invest your heart, your hustle, your energy, your passion, *but not your money*. So I asked my friend to help me. He had a video company and offered to come help me film my first video on his off time. I was terrible, but with his help, my first video launched. The worst thing I could have done was go out and buy a bunch of gear. What if I filmed two videos, found I didn't like it, and now had this expensive camera equipment taking up space in my basement? Try it once. See if you like it. Then find ways to keep going. My friend helped me make my first video, and I wasn't very good, but it was fun, and I wanted to continue. Now, he wasn't going to come every week to help me do this for free, so I needed to find another solution.

Break the problem down into the smallest next step.

What was my problem now? I needed a lot of things, but most important was a camera to film with. I asked all my friends if anyone had a camera I could borrow, and for my next videos I used their gear. I rotated between friends who had cameras and used theirs when they didn't need them. Then, as soon as I started making money, I bought the cheapest camera that would do the job. My first hundred dollars made on the channel went to buy my first camera.

Time to spray some gasoline!

With my own camera, I could film more regularly. I made more videos, I built more momentum, and I made more money, which I used to keep upgrading my cameras. I bought my cameras from Costco because they had the most generous return policy. If I didn't like it or use it, I could return it. I kept making videos. Then I looked at what I liked least about the whole process of making videos and found that I hated editing. I'd rather be in front of the camera and record the videos than spend all my time editing. So, as I started making money, my next investment was in a part-time editor. That hire let me go from making one video a week to one video per day! More videos led to more money, which let me make more investments. I hired that editor full time. Then I hired an assistant, then a researcher, then someone for community management, then a cameraman, then another editor, and so on. But it started with zero money.

Another great way to start with no money is with a service, not a product.

This was one of the first videos I shot myself using my friend's camera. Always face the window instead of having it behind you! Rookie mistake, but that's how you learn!

This one I shot on an old flip camera. I put it on my shelf and it kept wobbling, so this video footage is bouncing and hard to watch. Not perfect, but post it anyway!

START WITH A SERVICE FIRST

> "Whoever renders service to many puts himself
> in line for greatness—great wealth, great return,
> great satisfaction, great reputation, and great joy."
>
> —JIM ROHN

I believe most entrepreneurs are better off starting with a service.

Products are great because they are scalable. You aren't trading your time for money like you are in a service-based business. But there are two unique advantages of having a service that I think makes it the best starting point to make money from your purpose.

1. It gets you close to your customer.

Who is your customer? The person who is experiencing the same pain you went through. That's who you're going to help. So start talking to them. Start helping them. Start understanding them. The more you get to know them and get practice helping them overcome their struggles, the better you'll know what kind of product to sell to them. When you launch your product, you'll also have a customer base ready to help you. You're not creating in the dark, so it will dramatically improve the odds of your first product being a hit.

2. It's a faster way to make money.

It's faster to start a service, because you don't need anything. You've already got it. It's you. It's what's in your head. It's your experience. You saved yourself, and you can save others. That's something you can market and sell today. Products take more time to develop, create, produce, ship, and figure out logistics for. I want you making money as soon as possible. The faster you're making money, the faster you're out of your job, living your purposeful life, and helping more people.

What service do you offer? It's your *Recipe for Success* that we already covered. It's the exact steps that you followed to help you get out of your pain. It worked for you, and people will pay you for your advice on how to do it themselves. For example, the most basic version is a coaching/consulting program. It looks like this:

- You do a free call with people for twenty to thirty minutes. Blow them away with value so they want to talk with you again.
- Book another session, this time paid. If you're brand new and don't know what to charge, start with fifty dollars an hour. Offer an ongoing coaching program where they get six sessions with you for the price of five.
- As you get more clients, start raising your prices. Each time try raising it by another 30 percent.

As an example, let's help "The Concussion Man" become a six-figure consultant.

BUILDING A
$100,000 BUSINESS

"If you're trying to create a company, it's like baking
a cake. You have to have all the ingredients
in the right proportion."

—ELON MUSK

Remember Michael Edwards?

He was "The Concussion Man" who helped save my brain when I
had a concussion and broke my neck. His *Recipe for Success* is as
follows: twice a day, do healing meditations where you visualize
yourself getting better. His first call should be a free consultation
to understand what his customers are trying to heal. He then
should give them specific music to listen to and a set of instructions for how to do a healing meditation. Then he should demo
it with them. Really blow them away with value and make them
feel like there is hope. Then he can offer to give them another
call where he'll help them for an hour...or six sessions for the
price of five. Since Michael is brand new at this, he starts at fifty
dollars an hour, and as he gains more clients, confidence and
results, he slowly starts increasing his price. Every ten clients he

189

gets, he increases the price per hour again by 30 percent. Sound reasonable? Could you apply that same formula for yourself, teaching your *Recipe for Success*?

How does this get to you $100,000?

How much you make depends on two things: how much you're charging per session and how many sessions you're doing. Here's a list of how many paid one-hour sessions you would have to lead per week to get to $100,000.

The Path to $100,000+/Year	
Hourly Rate	Hours/Week Needed
$50	39
$75	26
$100	20
$150	13
$200	10
$250	8
$300	7

Think this is a lot to charge? As a comparison, lawyers cost between $150 an hour to upwards of $1,000 an hour. You're helping people solve a massive pain. Remember that as you get better and get more clients, you should charge more money. You deserve it. You've earned it. And with that money, you can help more people.

Awesome! But how can you find clients who will pay you?

THREE FREE WAYS TO GET CLIENTS

"Selling is something we do for our clients—
not to our clients."

—ZIG ZIGLAR

You don't need to spend big money on ads to get your first clients.

There are three key ways for you to get your first clients. Use these three ways to get enough money for you to quit your job, start making good money, and then expand into paid ways to spray gasoline on the fire of your business growth.

The first way is the *Fast Pass to Freedom*, where you'll be reaching out directly to ideal clients, showing your credibility, offering them value up front, and building your roster of paid clients. You could be making significant money this week if you just apply this method.

The second way is *partnerships and alliances*, where you reach out to people who are already selling to your target audience. Instead of having to go to customers one at a time, you talk with people who already know those people and can make the introduction for you. This method takes longer to apply, but when it comes through, your business will blast off!

The third way is *being a thought leader*, where you create content that becomes a marketing magnet, attracting ideal clients so you don't have to reach out to anyone. The clients just keep coming to you. This takes the most time to build, but it becomes an ongoing flow of income for you that only builds with time.

Let's start with the fastest way to make money, because I want you getting results as soon as possible.

Let me introduce you to the Fast Pass to Freedom!

3 FREE WAYS TO GET CLIENTS

"Happy clients are the best advertising money can buy."
- Anonymous

THE FAST PASS TO FREEDOM

"There is no easy walk to freedom anywhere, and many of us will have to pass through the valley of the shadow of death again and again before we reach the mountaintop of our desires."

—NELSON MANDELA

It's time for you to get your freedom!

You start the *Fast Pass to Freedom* by creating a digital place that showcases your expertise. You tell your story. You talk about your *Who*, *Why*, and *How*. The idea here is that if your ideal client came to this page, they would want to hop on a call with you. There are two main ways to do this.

The first is your website.

You don't need to have a fancy website that costs a lot of money to set up. You could have a single landing page. It needs to have your picture, your *Who*, *Why*, *How*, and an overview of your *Recipe for Success*. Coming to your page should make me feel like I'm going through exactly what you went through, and *you're* the person who can help me. Show me that you know what you're talking about. Bonus points if you want to include a video of yourself sharing your story. It can all fit on one simple page because people aren't hiring you for your design skills (unless they are, in which case your site had better look amazing). People are hiring you for what's in your head.

The second is social media.

Most social media platforms have the ability to add your picture, include a bio, and upload content. Again, the goal is that if an ideal client came to your profile page, they would want to talk with you. So let's make you look like you're the person to help them! Start with your picture. Make it good, because first impressions matter. Also, make sure it speaks to your target audience. If you're targeting lumberjacks, you probably don't want to be in a suit. If you're targeting CEOs, you probably don't want to be in your favorite sports team's jersey. Some other generic guidelines are: don't wear a hat or sunglasses, don't make your profile picture your logo, and make it a headshot so I can see the whites of your eyes. You might love your full body shots, but when people are loading it on their phones, they can't see you. It's too small. These guidelines don't apply in every situation, but be smart and think about your audience. Also, get a friend who knows what they're doing to help you. This one picture is going to do a lot of heavy lifting, so you want it to be good. Next is your bio. How much space you get varies depending on the platform, but every word must do work for you. Make me feel that you know what I'm going through. Give me hope. Help me understand that there is a path through the pain. Use all of the allowed space for your bio, and make every word count.

The most important step is next: uploading amazing content.

THE AMAZING CONTENT TEN-PACK

"If people believe in themselves, it's amazing
what they can accomplish."

—SAM WALTON

Great content is the next critical step to the *Fast Pass to Freedom.*

I want you to create a ten-pack of content. Create ten different pieces for the platform that give me answers, that help me, that provide insights. Each platform has its own approach, but it's usually a mix of pictures, videos, and text. Here is an easy way to break up the ten posts:

1. Your Who. Tell me your single most important core value, where it comes from, and why it's so important to you.

2. Your Why. Explain why you do what you do. Tell me your pain and how it led to your purpose.

3. Your How. Give me an overview of your *Recipe for Success* by telling me what steps you took to get out of your pain.

4–6. Recipe Breakdown. Take the three most important steps of your *Recipe for Success* and go deeper on each one.

7. Results. Tell me your results. Show me your transformation. Where did you come from, and *where* are you now?

8–9. Examples. Show me other people who are like me, and explain their transformation. Tell the stories of people you have helped directly or give hypothetical examples of how you would help someone if they came to you with specific problems.

10. Hope. Make me feel that it's possible for me as well—that if I connect with you and follow your advice, I too can solve my pain.

Spend some time thinking about these points. Hundreds (and soon thousands) of people are going to be seeing them, so make them as high quality as you can. And again, the most important part isn't how good it looks (unless you are a designer selling design services). The most important element is the information. Does the content make me *feel*? Does it make me *think*? Does it *resonate*? Does it make me *believe* that you can help me?

If so, then you're ready for the final step: outreach.

REACHING OUT TO PEOPLE

"Do not fear mistakes. You will know failure.
Continue to reach out."

—BENJAMIN FRANKLIN

**You've created great content, but it won't matter
if nobody sees it.**

You now need to get your message in front of the right people.
Your ideal clients need you. They are suffering. They're in pain.
And you can help. Let's go find them! The fastest way is through
people who self-identify on social media.

People share their lives on social media. They share what
they love. They share what they hate. They share what they're
struggling with. Many feel that people *over-share* on social
media. But that's actually a good thing for you because people
are sharing about the very thing that you can help them with.
Michael Edwards, "The Concussion Man," reached out to me to
help with my concussion because he saw me post about it on
social media. The graphic designer who I use for my Instagram
account reached out to me because he saw me post on social
media. People are posting. You just need to find them and reach
out. There are two ways to do it.

The first is search.

Search for keywords that relate to your area of expertise. Every social media platform has a search function. Who is posting about it? What are they struggling with? Can you help? If yes, reach out. For example, if Michael searched for "concussion" on YouTube, he might see a video uploaded yesterday called "I Got a Concussion Playing Hockey and May Not Be Able to Play Again." Reach out.

The second is hashtags.

All social media platforms at the time of this writing use hashtags. Hashtags are categories of content and are another way to sort and organize posts. Michael could look at "*#Concussion*" on any of the main platforms and find thousands of people talking about it every day. Reach out.

That's the *Fast Pass to Freedom.*

Create a website or profile with a great picture and bio. Create your ten-pack of amazing content that connects people to you. Then find your ideal clients and reach out to them. What are they going to do? Before they reply, they're going to look at your page and they're going to get inspired! That's why we did all that work creating a great page. Reach out to fifty potential ideal clients per day and offer the free call.

Here is exactly what to say.

USE THIS SCRIPT TO GET CLIENTS

"If you want to be successful, find someone who has achieved the results you want and copy what they do and you'll achieve the same results."

—TONY ROBBINS

Copy this template, update it for your expertise, and land your clients.

Subject (if email)/First line of message (if social): Getting You to (benefit)

Hi (first name),

My name is (your first name), and I saw that you are suffering from (their pain).

I'm so sorry to hear that, and I was moved by your story. I went through (the same pain) myself, thought it would never get better, but found a few simple yet powerful ways to solve it. Now I teach others how they can overcome (that issue) as well. You can check (my bio/my website) for a little more on my story. I've got three ideas for you that I think will really help, and I'd love to hop on a quick call with you to explain them to you. There is hope on the other side, and I'd love to help.

Much love,

(Your full name)

(A quote or tagline that embodies your Who)

Here's an example, using my Michael Edwards story:

Getting You Back to 100 Percent Brain Power!

Hi Evan,

My name is Michael, and I saw that you are suffering from a concussion.

I'm so sorry to hear that, and I was moved by your story. I went through four concussions myself and thought it would never get better, but found a few simple yet powerful ways to solve it. Now I teach others how they can overcome concussions as well. You can check my bio for a little more on my story. I've got three ideas for you that I think will really help, and I'd love to hop on a quick call with you to explain them to you for free. There is hope on the other side, and I'd love to help.

Much love,

Michael Edwards

"Whether you believe you can or you can't, you're right." (Henry Ford)

Powerful right? Make it your own. Start doing your fifty outreaches per day. Fifty might sound like a lot. Yes, it's work. But would you rather do work on your business or work for someone else? You could start making money today. Book your free calls. Give them value. Charge for follow-ups. Build your business. Change the world.

Now let's talk about another powerful strategy you can use to scale up quickly.

Here's the actual first message that Michael wrote to me when he found out about my injury. His was one of the only ones I could reply to because I couldn't focus on my phone or computer for too long with my concussion.

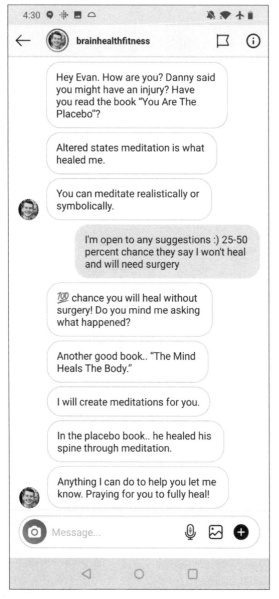

PARTNERSHIPS AND ALLIANCES

"I'm no longer an artist; I'm a business partner."

—PITBULL

The *Fast Pass to Freedom* relies on daily grunt work.

Create a great bio and picture. Make your ten-pack of amazing content. Then reach out to fifty ideal clients every day. If you want money in your pocket quickly, this is the path. If you want to quit your job to follow your passion, this is the answer. It's effective, but it takes a lot of daily work. It's much better than having a job working for someone else. But it's still a daily grind, because you're going after one person at a time.

If you want to level up your game, connect with potential alliance partners.

These are super-connectors. They're people that can get your message out to hundreds, thousands, or even millions of people. Instead of going after fifty new people every day like we did in the *Fast Pass to Freedom*, this strategy is to go after less than fifty people total—the fifty people that matter in your industry.

If you got one of them to endorse and recommend you, what would it mean to your business?

This plan is slow...and then really, *really* fast.

It takes time to build relationships. It takes time for people to know you. It takes time for them to like you, believe in you, and be willing to share your message. It's slow, frustrating, and you won't make money in the process (that's why you start with the *Fast Pass to Freedom*). But once you get a yes, it could make your entire business.

If you already know someone, reach out.

You may not know one of the top fifty that you ideally want. But maybe you know someone who can make a few introductions for you. Awesome—reach out! Tell them what you're up to. Again, your *Who, Why, How* story is going to be the thing that draws them in. Ask for help and see what they say. If they get you to your first few clients then they've shortcut your path. It's high leverage for you.

Maybe they'll help because they like you. Maybe they'll help because they owe you something. Maybe they'll help because they believe in your mission. Or maybe they just want to get paid and you'll give them a cut of what you make. Understand what motivates them and play to it. You're co-creating here so don't insist on only having one path. Some people might want a 30 percent commission. Some may ask for a favor in the future. Some may just want to help. Figure out what drives them and help them get it.

But what if you don't know anybody?

MY BIG MISTAKE WITH BANKERS

"I went to the bank and proposed that they lend money to the poor people. The bankers almost fell over."

—MUHAMMAD YUNUS

When I was in my first company, I didn't know anyone.

I was still in my teens, had never really run a business before, and had no idea what I was doing. So I went to my local bank. I thought that bankers helped entrepreneurs, so I booked a meeting. It ended up being such an awkward experience. I confidently walked in, sat down in the banker's office ready for him to explode my business, and here's how the conversation went:

Me: "*Thank you so much for seeing me! So, how can you guys help?*"

Him: "*Well, do you need a loan?*"

Me: "*Umm, I don't think so. I mean, I don't know. I just started my business and I came here for help. I don't really know what I'm doing.*"

Him: "*That's not really what we do here. We're a bank, so we give loans to small businesses to grow their companies.*"

Me: *"Ok, well maybe I need a loan. How does that work?"*

Him: *"If you haven't been in business for at least three years you'll have to personally guarantee the loan. It can't just be on your business."*

Me: *"I don't have any money yet. That's what I'm hoping my business can give me."*

Him: *"So you'll need to get someone to co-sign it and guarantee it for you. Maybe someone can help."*

Me: *"That's why I came here. I want to do it on my own."*

I went in feeling confident that my life and business were about to get a swift boost forward and walked out feeling like I got a swift boot to the face. You may feel like you have no connections and don't know how to reach out to your top fifty people.

Let me give you a strategy you can use to get anyone's attention.

GETTING BIG NAMES
TO SEE YOU

"Try not to become a man of success, but rather try to
become a man of value."

—ALBERT EINSTEIN

**At the core of every business relationship is *bringing
people value.***

The more value you bring clients, the more they'll pay you. The
more value you bring potential partners, the more they will recip-
rocate as well. The first step is having them know that you exist.

Start by hanging out where they hang out.

Doing this in person might be difficult. Chances are the places
where they hang out are private or are too expensive for you.
Maybe they have a speaking event you can attend or a meet-up
they're hosting. If you can get there, do it. But those are long shots,
and we need to get some guaranteed momentum. I've got good
news for you: the Internet has created unprecedented access.
Almost everyone you want to connect with is on social media.

Look for the platform where they are most involved.

Chances are your top fifty are on multiple social media platforms. But they're not giving equal time to each of them. Maybe their team is posting for them to Facebook. Maybe they're just duplicating content from their Instagram to all their other accounts. Don't look for where they are posting content. Instead, look for where they are *engaging* with people. Where are they *responding* to people? Where are they answering questions? Where are they asking questions and interacting with their followers? That's where you want to be. *Ignore all their other accounts* and just focus on that one. Their focus becomes your focus.

Be their best contributor.

Now that you know where they pay attention, you need to get on their radar. The goal here is not to be a fanboy or fangirl. The goal is to bring value to them and their community. If they ask a question, you give the most insightful answer of anyone. If someone asks them a question, you respond if they didn't. If they ask people to review their podcast, you give a meaningful review and tell others to help too.

You want to be a *known quantity*. When they see your picture, when they see your name, they know who you are. They recognize you. They are appreciative of you. That's the first step. Until they recognize and appreciate you, you're not ready.

Here's what happens in my community.

HOW TO SECURE BIG NAMES

1. HANG OUT
where they
hang out.

2. FIND THE
platform where
they're most
involved.

3. BE THEIR
best
contributor.

*"People are the most important thing. Business model
and product will follow if you have the right people."*
- Adam Neumann

HOW PEOPLE GET ON MY RADAR

"I walk by studio heads and they actually look
and put their hand out now, like maybe
I should be on their radar."

—ROBERT DOWNEY JR.

Most of the people who reach out to me are in ask, ask, ask mode.

Evan, can you answer this question of mine? Evan, can you review my website? Evan, can you check out my pitch deck and tell me what I'm missing? Evan, can you test my app? Evan, will you invest in my business? Evan, can you share my products and services with all of your fans and tell them how great I am? I promise I'll make it up to you...

That's not how it works.

Ninety-nine percent of people will ignore these kinds of messages. They don't know you. Don't reach out like that. There's no way you're getting a yes. You're wasting your time as well as theirs. That's not a great start to the relationship. I'll often reply with something like, "That's not how it works. Nobody is going to just promote you to their entire audience from a cold outreach without knowing you or your business. Here's what you want to do instead. Bring the people you're reaching out to so much value that they trip all over themselves to find a way to help you."

There are some people I'd do a lot for.

Many are people who I've never met in person, people who have never bought any of my products, people who have no money or connections to help me with. But I know them because they are insanely valuable to my community. They don't have money, but they put in the time. They show up to my live streams. They help other people in my community. They comment on everything I put up. They use their talents to try to help me. If any of them wrote to me asking for help with something, I'd do my best to do it. I couldn't guarantee I could do it, but I would try.

I've already done ten separate joint ventures with people in my community.

We're in business together. They turned their love of my work into a money-making venture with me. There are countless other people I've promoted, shouted out, and given exposure to because they did something that was worth talking about. And that's the key. You have to do something worth talking about. The bigger the name you're going after, the more work you're going to have to do to stand out because more people are chasing their attention. I was a lot easier to get to a couple of years ago compared to now. It'll only get harder in the coming years. Not impossible. Just harder. You put in the work. You get noticed. Then you ask.

But what if they're not on social media?

NINJA WAYS
TO GET TO PEOPLE

"I started out as a young Ninja and killed all of the Shoguns. I am a Shogun now and I'm holding my spot. There probably won't be another Shogun after this."

—SHAQUILLE O'NEAL

Not everyone is on social media.

I think social media is the most level playing field. You don't have to have money or connections to participate. If you pay attention, bring value, and stay consistent, you will get noticed.

(A quick note for any readers who aren't on social media themselves: You're hurting your business. It doesn't mean you need to share everything about your life. You also don't need to waste time consuming content you don't care about. Social media is a powerful tool, and if you aren't using it, you're running a race with both of your legs tied. You'll move, but very slowly. Whatever your aversion to social media is, you must overcome it. There is a solution if you'd just be willing to look. Find it. It's required.)

And what if the person you want to reach isn't on social media?

Then you get resourceful. If you're stuck on the side of the road, you use your cell phone to call for help, but if your cell is dead, you find another solution. That's what entrepreneurs do. We're resourceful. We find solutions to things that other people don't see. We don't give up easily. You can't give up easily.

You need to find a shared connection.

If you can't get to the person, then work on getting to the "person who knows the person." Map out who knows the target person you want to connect with, and then create a plan to reach out to them. It's going to be a lot more difficult, but if you feel it's worth it, it's totally possible. Here are some things to look for:

- What companies has she invested in?
- What charities does she work with?
- Who has she co-authored books with?
- Who are the suppliers she works with?
- Is anyone in her family in the public eye and on social media?
- Is she on the board of directors of any businesses?
- What hobbies does she have?
- What sports teams does she follow?
- What college/university did she go to?

I used these strategies to get to one of my heroes.

MY PLAN TO GET
HOWARD SCHULTZ

"When you're surrounded by people who share a
passionate commitment around a common purpose,
anything is possible."

—HOWARD SCHULTZ

Howard Schultz is the billionaire entrepreneur behind Starbucks.

The moment that turned me on to him was when he was at a shareholders' meeting just after Starbucks came out as one of the first big companies to support same-sex marriage. As a result of the announcement, the National Organization for Marriage launched a boycott against Starbucks. An angry shareholder challenged him at the meeting and said, "In the first full quarter after this boycott was announced, our sales and our earnings, shall we say politely, were a bit disappointing."

I was expecting a typical public-company CEO, boring, safe, say-nothing answer. Instead, Howard responded with:

"Not every decision is an economic decision. Despite the fact that you recite statistics that are narrow in time, we did

provide a 38 percent shareholder return over the last year. I don't know how many things you invest in, but I would suspect not many things, companies, products, investments have returned 38 percent over the last twelve months. Having said that, it is not an economic decision to me. The lens in which we are making that decision is through the lens of our people. We employ over 200,000 people in this company, and we want to embrace diversity. Of all kinds. If you feel, respectfully, that you can get a higher return than the 38 percent you got last year, it's a free country. You can sell your shares in Starbucks and buy shares in another company. Thank you very much."

My mind was blown. What CEO talks like that? I loved it.

And then I read his book, *Onward.*

I was in the process of writing my first book, *Your One Word*. The thesis of that book is that every human has one main core value, and you should find yours and bring it to your business. On page four of Howard's book, I read the following sentence and freaked out: "There is a word that comes to my mind when I think about our company and our people. That word is 'love.' I love Starbucks because everything we do is steeped in humanity." Whhhaaattt? Howard Schultz has *one word* and built Starbucks around it? In my book I was giving examples of companies that built their business around one word, and now I wanted to interview and include him in the book. There were two main problems. I was on a tight deadline, and I didn't know Howard.

Time to get to work.

*Yes, I'm a big Howard Schultz and **Onward** fan! His picture is on one of five big canvases hanging on my office wall.*

GOING NINJA
ON HOWARD SCHULTZ

"I think if you're an entrepreneur, you've got to dream
big and then dream bigger."

—HOWARD SCHULTZ

I made it my mission to get in touch with Howard Schultz for my book.

My default first step was going to social media. Twitter was my favorite, since I seemed to always get the highest response rate from people there. Howard was the CEO of a giant company. *This should be an easy one*, I thought. *Let me go to Twitter and get on his radar.*

Wait...Howard Schultz is not on Twitter?

I honestly couldn't believe it. Everyone in the business world is on Twitter. They might not be super active, but they at least have an account. Not Howard. Ok, Instagram? Nope. YouTube? Nada. Wow. All right, no problem. I'll just work my connections. Someone has to have a connection that can put me in touch, if not with Howard, then with someone who knows him. Strike two. Again, it was another shock. Usually, if it's in the business community, I can find someone who knows someone and get an introduction. It was a humbling moment to realize that my network wasn't as good as I thought it was! So it was time to go old school, which I hadn't done in a while—like using a sundial instead of a clock to tell time.

Who does Howard hang with?

My team and I started making a list of every possible connection that we could think of. We did a ton of outreach but were most confident about three in particular. The first was Maveron, a venture capital firm. Howard invested in the company and was a co-founder. He's investing in entrepreneurs. Right up my alley! The second was going directly to Starbucks PR. I've got a big audience. I'm writing a book with a major publisher. Their PR department should be interested in this and could at least get me a meeting. The third was Joanne Gordon. She was the ghost-writer for *Onward*, the book where I found the line that sent me on this mission in the first place!

The third option ended up becoming my best option.

I couldn't make inroads with the venture-capital company. Starbucks PR wasn't returning my messages. None of the other leads I investigated were working. If I had six months or more to do this, I would have made a breakthrough, but I was on a deadline from my publisher. This was a last-minute addition. We didn't have time for it, but I was determined to get in. And after I wrote a cold email to Joanne, she replied with a message of hope that something could happen!

Here's the letter I wrote to her.

THE LETTER THAT GOT AN INTRODUCTION

Hi Joanne,

This might be one of the stranger emails you receive today...

My name is Evan Carmichael. I have a popular website that over twenty million people have visited and a rapidly growing YouTube channel with over five million views. I also have a radio show that reaches almost 600 stations across America, and *Forbes* named me one of the "Top 40 Social Marketing Talents." I'm doing an interview series and am writing a book with a major publisher called One Word, where I'm discussing finding one word that you believe in to your core, and profiling entrepreneurs who have built businesses around their one word. After reading *Onward* (amazing, amazing, AMAZING book)... did I say amazing? :) .... I noticed these lines: "There is a word that comes to my mind when I think about our company and our people. That word is 'love.' I love Starbucks because everything we do is steeped in humanity." Howard Schultz is one of my favorite entrepreneurs of all time because he has an important mission and he really stands for something powerful. It's inspiring, and I wish every entrepreneur knew about his story so they could model him and learn from him. My question for you is if there is any way you'd be able to set up an introduction to him to see if I could interview him for my series and my book. I know it's a huge ask, especially coming from a complete stranger...and it's totally outside my usual style of doing things, but I don't have any other connections at the moment. I don't know that I have much to offer you in return apart from a heartfelt thank you and lifelong gratitude. I'd be happy to help promote projects that you're working on to my audience. I don't know if that's important to you and really hate the idea of just trading favors. I guess the bottom line is, I would really appreciate an introduction and I would be in lifelong debt to you, happy to help whenever I can, whenever you need, because you did something lovely for a complete stranger who is trying to do something important and powerful for the world. I'm happy to provide you with more information on me, the series, the book.

Thank you so much for your consideration and your time. I sincerely appreciate it.

Cheers,

Evan

#Believe.

WHAT DID JOANNE SAY?

"Thank you for such a heartfelt and sincere email..."

—JOANNE GORDON

Joanne saw my email and replied with:

Hi Evan,

Thank you for such a heartfelt and sincere email. I am touched that the book resonated with you the way it did. And no, you can never say "amazing" enough to an author. :-) I have shared your email with the powers that be at Starbucks who handle requests such as yours for Howard. Someone will reach out to you, and hopefully you will get your meeting.

Thanks again for emailing and congratulations on all of your success.

Best,

Joanne

Twelve days later I got an email from Starbucks:

Hi Evan,

I hope you are well! My name is [removed for privacy reasons] and I work on the Public Affairs team at Starbucks. Joanne forwarded us your email. It was so nice to see your passion about *Onward*! I worked closely with Joanne and Howard on the book, and to use your word—it was an "AMAZING" book and project to get to be a part of!

Would I actually be able to get an interview with Howard for my book?

WHAT DID STARBUCKS SAY?

"There's always a way."

—ALEX BANAYAN

So there's good news and bad news.

The bad news is I didn't get the interview in time. I was introduced to the head of global PR at Starbucks, the person who decides what gets to Howard and what doesn't. She said the book concept was interesting but Howard had to be the one to speak on it. Nobody else could comment, because it was Howard's "one word." And unfortunately he was tied up over the period that I had open before my book deadline.

The good news is that I got the momentum.

I just ran out of time. Alex Banayan has a strategy called the "third door." The idea is that when you're trying to do something difficult, the front door to the house you want to get into is usually locked. The window is locked too. So you have to find the third door. You have to find another way in. I spent all that time messaging and trying to get in touch with Starbucks PR and barely made a difference. And then, by sending a heartfelt letter to the ghostwriter of Howard's book, I got an introduction right to the top. Third door.

Here's why I lost: I went right to the ask.

I wasn't her *Chief Goal Officer*. I didn't know what she wanted. I didn't build a relationship. I didn't create rapport. I didn't provide value. I went in completely cold. I had to because of the timeline. Sometimes that's just how it goes. You'll run out of time.

That's why you start with the *Fast Pass to Freedom*.

You create ten pieces of amazing content and reach out to fifty ideal targets every day to start making money. You don't want to run out of time in your business. If you go all in on your company, then the time limit is how much is in your bank account. Once you're out of money, you have to go back to getting a job. If the partner you're trying to land doesn't come through for you in time, you can't let it be fatal to your business.

I still launched my book without Howard.

It would have been the sweetest bonus and a dream come true for me to get an interview with him. But I still had a great book that I was incredibly proud of. Use the *Fast Pass to Freedom* to build your base, have stable income, and keep your business alive. Then layer partnerships and alliances on top like you'd add sprinkles and whipped cream on your cupcakes.

And then you're ready for the third strategy to get clients: content thought-leadership.

YOU ARE A THOUGHT LEADER

"We all have a life story and a message that can inspire
others to live a better life or run a better business.
Why not use that story and message to serve others
and grow a real business doing it?"

—BRENDON BURCHARD

This is the most effective long-term marketing strategy.

So far everything we've talked about is outbound. You're writing
to potential clients. You're trying to get on the radar of influential people. There's a third strategy that beats both of them. The
problem is, it takes the longest to win at. Most people who try
this strategy give up because they don't give it enough time—
plus they often don't incorporate the first two strategies to make
sure they have money coming in to support their short-term
growth. You can't focus on the long term if you're not eating
in the short term. The third strategy is being a thought leader
and using content marketing to bring a steady stream of quality
clients right to you without ever having to do a single sales call.

What's a thought leader?

Being a thought leader means you're an expert. You've got ideas
and strategies that can help people. You have a *How* and a *Recipe*

for Success. You lead with your *Who*, and you're doing it because of your *Why.* As a result, you're a weird duck. You see the world differently than others. And if you can teach others to think like you think, you can make a huge impact and make a lot of money automatically.

At the core of this strategy is creating content.

Many people are going through the pain you went through, and they're searching for answers. They're going online. They're looking. They'll now find you, because you're posting solutions. In the *Fast Pass to Freedom* you need to create a ten-pack of content. It's great content that will make your ideal clients want to work with you. But to get those clients to see it, you need to message people every day. In the thought leader strategy, instead of reaching out to clients, you create content every day. You're not just making ten pieces of great content. You're making tons of great content. It gets seen because, eventually, if you keep posting amazing content, you reach critical mass where the social media networks start promoting you. You start building an audience. You become a brand name within your industry. You get known, and the more you get known, the more your message spreads, the more clients come to you, and the more opportunities come your way. Eighty percent of winning on social media is creating amazing content daily. If you're not gaining a following it's because either you're not posting every day or the content isn't amazing. Yet. Getting traction is a painful, slow process, but I'm going to make it easier for you. Since it's the hardest marketing strategy to win at, I'm going to go into more detail to help you.

It starts with picking the right platform.

STOP TRYING
TO BE EVERYWHERE

"Do not try to do everything. Do one thing well."

— STEVE JOBS

The common advice in marketing is to be on every social media platform.

Stop that. You're not dedicating enough time to be great everywhere, and you're trying to run a business, not be on social media all day long. You're posting mediocre content everywhere that nobody cares about. Would you subscribe to you on these platforms? If you're not putting out content that you're proud of, stop. Immediately.

Here's what you should do instead.

Start by getting accounts everywhere. Get the account so nobody can take your name. Yes, put your picture up. Put your bio up. Post your ten-pack of content. Do the steps from the *Fast Pass to Freedom*. Then stop...and listen. You're going to pick one social media platform to start with and dominate; the other ones you're going to use for *listening*. If Twitter isn't your number one, then you just listen on Twitter. *Listening* just means that when someone mentions you, you reply.

Next, recognize your champions.

You don't need to do anything on Twitter (or any other platform) to get results. If someone mentions you and you get the notification, thank them. You don't need a Twitter content strategy. Just recognize your champions. First, it just makes business sense. If someone mentions you, you should know what they're saying. You should be a part of the conversation. If you have an opportunity to be a part of a dialogue where people are talking about your business online, you should do it. Second, the people who are talking about you have audiences of their own. And if you thank them for mentioning you, what do you think is going to happen? They'll do it more! You may never build an audience on that platform, but if you just say thank you and recognize the people who like your work, you'll keep building awareness for your business and message. It takes very little time to do. You won't be getting bombarded by notifications on platforms you're not involved in. Get your name locked up so nobody can take it from you, and listen so you can recognize your champions. That should be your strategy for every social media network except one.

Next, pick one platform and get ready to dominate.

PICK THE BEST
SOCIAL MEDIA PLATFORM

"The possibilities are numerous once we decide
to act and not react."

—GEORGE BERNARD SHAW

So how do you pick the social media platform that's best for you?

It comes down to a combination of where your ideal customers are and what you're great at. It's Marketing 101: be where your customers are. If you help redheaded women and there's a festival for redheaded women happening in Dallas, you want to go to Dallas. You need to be in the right room. Every social media platform has a different demographic and intent. For example, at the time of this writing, LinkedIn is a great place to connect with business professionals. On the other hand, if you are targeting young people, you need to be on Instagram.

Next, what are you great at?

Creating content falls into three buckets: video, audio, and the written word. Every social media network values these three buckets differently. What do you love doing? Would you rather record a video, make an audio broadcast, or write an article? Don't force yourself to do something you hate. Mix the thing that you love doing with where your audience is. For example, I love making videos. I write books when I have a lot to say on a topic and it fits the format, but most of my content is video. I love video. I love the impact of my videos. I love seeing the videos come to life. And at the time of this writing, YouTube is the biggest platform for videos.

My audience of entrepreneurs is on YouTube, so that's my primary home. If the demographics of the platforms change, which they do as people get older and culture shifts, we will have to change. I may not be doing YouTube in ten years. I probably won't. But remember, 80 percent of winning the social media game is creating amazing content daily. Learn how to do it on one platform, and if that platform goes away, at least you gained the skill set. Eighty percent of what you learned will still be relevant, and you can dominate on the next network.

Love writing and speaking to the technical crowd? Get on Medium. Want to make short videos and connect with Millennials? Instagram is your home. Love creating long videos with a broad message? YouTube is your best bet. Would you rather interview people and release audio-only content? Start a podcast. Every few years, the networks change. The audience changes. The popularity changes. Don't let it scare you. Adjusting is not that difficult. If you're focused on one platform at a time and you learn how to make great content, you're going to win.

Let me show you how to make great thought-leadership content.

HOW TO START ON SOCIAL

1 GET YOUR ACCOUNT NAME ON EVERY PLATFORM TO **PROTECT THE NAME.**

2 PUT UP YOUR **PICTURE, BIO, & A 10-PACK** OF CONTENT.

3 LISTEN TO, AND **RECOGNIZE, YOUR CHAMPIONS.**

4 **PICK ONE PLATFORM** ONLY TO DOMINATE ON.

MAKE ME THINK
LIKE YOU THINK

"We are shaped by our thoughts.
We become what we think."

— BUDDHA

You've got one job as a thought leader: make me think like you think.

Most thought-leadership content sucks. It's not converting. The message is not getting out there, usually because the format isn't working. Most people create content that starts with something like this, "Hey guys, welcome back! It's me, Jimmy, and today I want to talk you about something I've been thinking about for a long time. It's great to see you again so let's get into this now and start talking about...."

No!

You haven't said anything yet. Nothing. People won't give you that much time to get your message out. You need to hit them immediately. You must lead with your powerful opinion. Make them feel and think something powerful from your very first sentence. You need to capture them with the way you think and pull them in so they want to learn more. Your content is not for your friends. It's for your ideal clients. You have ideas that can save them. You need to pull those ideas out of you and give them to the world. Your friends will have patience. Your friends want to see what you're doing. Your friends care about your updates. People who don't know you don't care. Your content needs to have a message. I need to be transformed by the message. Your stories need to teach me about myself and give me a new perspective.

You have something important to say.

You've been through pain. You have a purpose. You want to serve. Before you start creating thought-leadership content, remember what the intent is. You're trying to shift someone's perspective and give them hope. When you're in front of someone, it's much easier. You see them. You feel them. You understand them. It's hard to be at home in front of just your plants and record a fantastic video with emotion that will move people. But that's the job. That's the skill you need to learn. To achieve it, the best thing to do is imagine you're helping someone. Either imagine yourself helping the person you were, or imagine helping someone who is going through pain right now. Not some fictitious person—it has to be relevant to you. If you want to deliver an emotional message, you need to be emotionally tied to this person. It needs to be someone you know, someone you've met, someone you care for. Imagine that person. Picture them in your head. And then create an epic piece of thought-leadership content that speaks directly to them. Speak to that person and change their life. You have something important to say that can deeply and profoundly impact people, and it's time to get that message out.

Let me show you what the perfect thought-leader content structure looks like.

I've used these strategies to build my own YouTube channel to two million subscribers and hundreds of millions of views, as well as to consult for some of the biggest names in the industry. Now it's your turn!

THE PERFECT THOUGHT-LEADER CONTENT

"I think that structure is required for creativity."

—TWYLA THARP

Follow this structure and you'll start making the impact you're after.

1. First sentence is a powerful opinion. Hit me in the gut right away. Don't welcome me. Don't tell me about your day. Don't give me an intro. You've got five seconds before you lose me. Lead with a powerful opinion, and make me pay attention.

2. Second sentence is context. You just said something bold. Now, give some context around it—one extra sentence to make it make a little more sense.

3. Third sentence is to raise the stakes. Make me feel the pain if I don't act now. What happens if I don't listen to your advice? Move me from should to must.

4. Tell me a story that backs up your powerful opinion. It could be your story, the story of a client, something in the news, etc. People learn through stories, so tell me one that I can relate to.

5. (Advanced) Address the hedge. By now some people will be connected to you, but others will still be resistant. They haven't bought in yet that you understand them. They have fears, insecurities, and doubts. What will their reaction be to what you've just said? You can address these questions before moving on to the advice. To prime yourself, imagine someone you know hearing what you just said and then saying, "Yeah but...." Address the hedge. Show me that my "yeah buts" don't make sense, and that I need to pay attention to you.

6. Deliver your advice. You've told me something powerful. You've made me feel the pain to act now. You've given me a story so it makes more sense. You've addressed my rebuttals. Great! Now I'm with you. How do I fix it? Give me three tangible, specific, clear action items. Teach me what you know. You can't lead with the solution. I'm not emotionally committed to solving it yet. I'm not sold on you yet. But by point six, I am ready, so now tell me how to solve my problem with specific steps.

7. Bring it home. Finally, reinforce the opinion. Show me you care. Give me hope. Then tell me where I can reach you or what my next step with you should be.

That's it! The perfect thought-leadership content structure. Step five is advanced because applying it takes practice. It's not something you're going to be great at from the start. So when you're just getting going, skip this step. As you get better, challenge yourself by adding it in.

Let me give you an example of what your powerful opinion should look like.

STEPS 1–3:
YOUR POWERFUL OPINION

"You take the front line when there is danger.
Then people will appreciate your leadership."

—NELSON MANDELA

Remember, this is the structure for a persuasive opening three lines.

1. First sentence is a powerful opinion.
2. Second sentence is context.
3. Third sentence is to raise the stakes.

Let's say you want to inspire people to believe in their bold ideas:

1. *Powerful opinion*: "The decisions you make when you're feeling bold are actually the right ones for you but your head talks you down from following them."
2. *Context*: "When you're bold, confident, excited, feeling unstoppable, and you make a decision to get to the next level, that's actually the right decision for you."

3. *Raise the stakes*: "You have to listen to your boldness and take action, otherwise you'll live the rest of your life in regret, knowing you could have done something great but were too afraid to just go for it."

Or maybe you want people to raise their standards:

1. *Powerful opinion*: "If you want to raise your standards, you need to raise your environment."
2. *Context*: "Everything you're surrounded by keeps you where you are: your friends, your family, the media you consume, your habits, everything."
3. *Raise the stakes*: "Your environment has been perfectly created to prevent you from growing, and unless you decide to make a radical change today, you'll fall back into a mediocre life."

Apply this formula to the issues you talk about. Think about your *Why* and the problems you had in getting through the pain you suffered. I talk about believing in bold ideas and raising standards because I struggled with believing in my ideas. The lessons are personal because your purpose comes from your pain. What does the person you used to be need to hear from the person you are today? What is the powerful opinion they must understand? Lead with that!

But what if you're not 100 percent sure?

HOW TO MANAGE
YOUR DOUBTS

"Don't wait until you have enough facts to be
100 percent sure, because by then it is almost always
too late. Procrastination in the name of reducing risk
actually increases risk."

—COLIN POWELL

Colin Powell had an important rule he followed to make decisions.

Being a four-star general in the United States Army, he was responsible for a lot of heavy decisions. Making the wrong call would cost people's lives. He came up with the "Forty–Seventy Rule" to help him make decisions. When he was under 40 percent sure of an outcome, it was too reckless to go for. When he was over 70 percent sure, his window to act had likely closed. When he was between 40 and 70 percent sure, that's when he had to decide, and he went with his gut.

I use the 85 percent rule.

When I'm 85 percent sure on something, I act like I'm 100 percent. I don't just act like it—I am it. I'm 100 percent sure in my advice. I prefer 85 percent because we're not in an ever-changing battlefield against ever-changing enemies like Powell was. The pain you went through is mostly still the same for people today as it was for you back then. The *Recipe for Success* that you came up with works because what was relevant for you then is still relevant now. Sure, the technology might change, but the principals and the methods are the same. All you need to do is have the pattern recognition to know where people are in the process. The more people you see and help, the faster you'll figure out the pattern. Therefore, you can afford to jump to a higher percentage than Powell could. And when you're 85 percent certain, you need to be 100 percent. Here's why: the people you're helping have doubts, just like you used to. They aren't sure there even is a solution, let alone one that you can help them with. If they sense doubt in you, then they'll hold on to that doubt. Even though you will only be at the worst case 15 percent in doubt, that's what they'll hear because that's what they want to hear, and so they won't take action.

You will never be 100 percent certain.

The only way to know an outcome for sure is by looking backwards after you have already tried and failed or succeeded. You can't predict the outcome with 100 percent certainty going forward, ever. But if you're trying to help someone, you need to be certain for both of you. They're listening to you because they believe in how certain you are. Your certainty gives them hope. People often have a hard time speaking in black-and-white terms, but if you tone down your message, you tone down your impact. Pick opinions you are at least 85 percent certain of and give me the confidence that if I follow your advice, I'll get results.

Give me your powerful opinion then tell me a story to make it stick.

THE 85% RULE - EXPLAINED

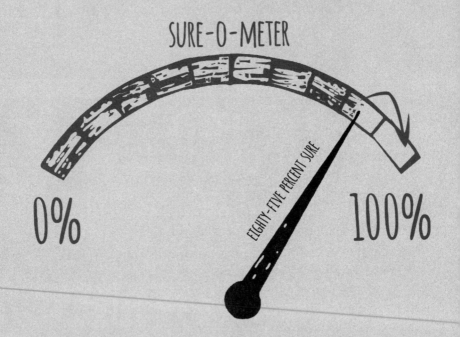

SURE-O-METER

EIGHTY-FIVE PERCENT SURE

0%   100%

*"When I'm 85% sure on something, I act like I'm 100%.
I don't just act like it, I am it. 100% sure in my advice."*
- Evan Carmichael

STEP 4:
TELL ME A STORY

"Your goal in every communication is to influence your target audience (change their current attitudes, belief, knowledge, and behavior). Information alone rarely changes any of these. Research confirms that well-designed stories are the most effective vehicle for exerting influence."

—KENDALL HAVEN

Telling a story is one of the most effective ways to influence someone.

Good stories build familiarity and trust. I see myself in your story and feel I'm just like who you were. Because you've now introduced me to a familiar world, I'm more open to learning. Stories are also more engaging than dry facts, and it's that emotional connection people make to you that will make them care long before they'll listen to your advice.

What kind of stories can you tell?

Start with your own, and don't summarize. Don't just give me a series of facts. Instead, make me feel like I'm sitting right next to you while it's happening. It's the difference between looking at your car going by on the street and being in the car with you as you're driving. Bring me into your story and make me feel how you feel. Tell me what's going through your mind and the impact it's having on you. Those are the stories that will influence people.

Here are some other ideas for stories you can tell:

- What you went through and how you overcame it, or what you are currently going through/struggling with.
- What you want to go through with, but are afraid of.
- What a friend/family member of yours faced or is facing (I'll often change the name, gender, and relationship to me if it's a sensitive story so it doesn't identify the person. The story matters more than the main character's identity).
- What's happening in the news that relates to your powerful opinion?
- Questions that are coming in from your audience or customers.
- Someone you met recently that made you reflect.
- A movie, song, sporting event, conference, rally, festival, vacation, business trip, concert, restaurant, event, etc. that you experienced and can share.

Powerful opinion. Then story. Then, if you're up for the challenge, address the hedge.

STEP 5:
ADDRESS THE HEDGE

"Persuasion is achieved by the speaker's personal character when the speech is so spoken as to make us think him credible."

—ARISTOTLE

Uncertainty kills action.

If you are uncertain as the thought leader, people won't follow your advice. That's why, when you're 85 percent certain, you must be 100 percent. As the people you're trying to help are consuming your content, they will also have their own uncertainty. They will have questions that you haven't answered, and unless you answer those questions, they'll hold on to that doubt as proof that your advice won't work.

You need to get into their head and squash the uncertainty.

How will people react to your message? What will they say? The more you practice and deliver your opinions, the more feedback you'll get that you can pour into your advice. Imagine you've just delivered your message, then complete these sentences for what the feedback would be:

- *"Yeah but, _____."*
- *"Maybe that works for you, however, _____."*
- *"You don't understand me, I'm _____."*
- *"Does that still work if _____?"*
- *"It's not that simple because _____."*

In a face-to-face conversation, you'll get the opportunity to answer questions. When you're creating thought-leadership content to build your brand, you won't.

Assume they have questions and answer them inside your content.

For each powerful opinion, go through those five questions and ask yourself what is the most likely objection people will have. Then address it in the content. You don't need to cover every single possible objection. Otherwise, people will tune out and leave. Pick the most likely one, and answer it head on.

Another way to deal with the hedge is the 85 percent rule. If you're up to 15 percent uncertain, what is the cause of that uncertainty? What's causing you to want to hedge your opinion and not be so black-and-white in your advice? Address that here. This is your chance to address the hedge. Give yourself permission to be bold at the start because you know you'll have this section here to talk about the resistance to the idea and handle objections.

Now you need to tell me what to do.

STEP 6:
DELIVER YOUR ADVICE

"We are not here to curse the darkness,
but to light the candle that can guide us through
the darkness to a safe and sane future."

—JOHN F. KENNEDY

**Now we get to the solutions. This is what you
wanted to do the whole time.**

Solve the problem. Everything we've done so far is the emotional
work to get people to feel connected to you, to snap them out of
their regular way of thinking and make them open to change.
They're ready; now you're going to give them the goods.

Think of three specific steps. Break this down and make
it easy to get started. What exactly am I supposed to do? For
example, go back to my powerful opinion example: "If you want
to raise your standards, you need to raise your environment."
Let's look at what my three actionable pieces of advice would be:

1. **Find your *Who*.** If you want to raise your standards, you
   need to first figure out what you're going to build your
   standards around. At the core, it should be based on your

247

Who, your most important value. It's not just who you are but who you aspire to be. My *Who* is #Believe, so I want to raise my standards on how much I #Believe in myself. To figure out what your *Who* is, think about one core value that you have that's more important than everything else. The core value defines you, and if someone asked you who you are in one word, this would be your answer.

2. ***Create an environment around your Who***. Think about where you spend most of your time and then elevate that environment to fit with your *Who*. I wanted more #Believe in my life, so I created giant canvas prints of my parents and my favorite entrepreneurs to hang on my wall. As soon as I walk into my office, they are staring me in the face, reminding me to #Believe in myself. Think about what's on your wall, your desk, your cell phone and desktop backgrounds, in your car, your wallet, and anything else you look at consistently. Then design it with intention to remind you to play a bigger game. You set it up once and it reminds you every day automatically to step up and be who know you can be.

3. ***Establish a morning routine to lift you up***. You are what you consistently do. You need to start your day with the thing that makes you feel your *Who*. For me, it's reminding myself that the work I do matters and then sharing a quick message to my audience online. If you start your day with the thing that made you feel bold, powerful, and unstoppable every day, your life will look dramatically different one year from today.

Make the advice specific, actionable, and easy to do. Now, bring it home!

STEP 7:
BRING IT HOME

"The true competitors are the ones who play to win."

—TOM BRADY

This is your last chance to deliver the win.

You've done everything right. You've given me a powerful opinion that interrupted my thought process and made me pay attention to you. You gave me more context so it makes more sense. Then, you raised the stakes and made me want to turn this *should* into a *must*. You gave me a story that was emotional and made me feel connected to you. It made me feel like you know what I'm going through and that you can help. And you addressed the hedge. You recognized where I'd feel skeptical, and now I'm ready to listen to you. And holy cow, that actionable advice was amazing and I'm taking it all in!

Here's how you close strong.

Reiterate what you told me. Remind me of the powerful opinion and why it's so important that I act now. And then make me feel like I can do it. Give me hope that all I need to do is get started on your advice today, and I'll start building momentum towards solving my problem. You've just opened my eyes and I'm excited to change my life for the better.

Now tell me what's next.

What do I do next? Do I watch another video of yours? Do I contact you for coaching? Do I buy your book? Do I join your newsletter list? Do I sign up for your free bonus? Do I attend your event? Do I subscribe or follow your social account? Tell me what I'm supposed to do. More than just the advice, I want that energy from you. I want that hope from you. I want it consistently. Because tomorrow I'm going to wake up and be the person I was before I met you, so I need to feel like you're with me on this journey. Make me hungry to stay with you.

And you're done!

That's the perfect thought-leadership content structure. You can adapt it for different platforms. For example, that entire process could be a ten- or fifteen-minute YouTube video. Or, if you only have fifteen seconds to do an Instagram story, just do the first three sentences. Adjust depending on the context, but practicing that structure is a skill you'll take with you for life. Your goal as a thought leader is to be able to tell a story in every context—whether it's a fifteen-second Instagram clip, a ten-minute YouTube video, or a thirty-minute keynote presentation to a three-day workshop. You want to be able to expand and contract your opinion and your message to fit the context. Practice. You'll change the world with your message.

"But I'm giving my advice away for...free?"

THOUGHT-LEADER TEMPLATE

1. POWERFUL OPINION

2. CONTEXT

3. STAKES

4. STORY

5. HEDGE

6. ADVICE

People suck at comunication. They fail to listen, fail to articulate, and **fail to connect.** It causes slow progress at best & fights, conflict —**even wars**— at worst. **A client asked me to help her bring a project to life** recently. We were blazing through it together, until we got to step seven, at which point she said "all this content will be great for my new e-course!" This was a problem, because just yesterday, she'd agreed to focus on current clients and back-burner the e-course. Her business didn't need e-courses, it needed happy clients & instant revenue. She totally dismissed our previous chat. Now, **you might say that's "no big deal",** but she'd spent the whole day working on an e-course instead of making money. Now think about how many conversations we have in our lives. Think about how much time is wasted on projects due to poor communication. It scales hard. Bad convos seem like no big deal, but walking and talking are the backbone of all we do. Inefficiencies here kill dreams. To fix it **you've got to X, Y, and Z...** and ta-da, **your dreams move forward at warp-speed.**

7. BRING IT HOME

"That's the perfect thought leadership content structure. You can adapt it for different platforms. "
- Evan Carmichael

THE FREE LEADS YOU
TO THE MONEY

"A large social-media presence is important because it's
one of the last ways to conduct cost-effective marketing.
Everything else involves buying eyeballs and ears.
Social media enables a small business to earn
eyeballs and ears."

—GUY KAWASAKI

Your first job is to get attention.

When you have attention, when people know you, when you're
seen as the expert, that's when you start getting paid. Give all
your advice away for free. Tell people exactly what they should
be doing and how. Make your content so valuable that you are
the go-to person for your industry and you get known for it.

So what are people paying for, then? *Access.* They're paying
for the one-on-one time with you. They want specific help. They
want to ask you their burning questions. They want your advice
to be tailored to them and what they're going through. They
want to be closer to you because you've done what they want to
do, and the more they're around you, the more they feel like it's
possible to do it as well. So, the more you create amazing content

that inspires people that hope is possible, the more people will pay you to help them achieve their goals.

Understand that most people won't pay you.

And that's great. It will only be a small percentage of people who ever ask you for coaching, buy your books, pay to see you speak, sign up for your program, etc. But the free people *lead* you to the paid people. Some people value money over time and others value time over money. The people who value time more than money want access to the experts. You have the answers and they'll pay you to help them. The people who value money over time won't buy from you, but they'll watch every video you put out and read every article you publish. The more eyeballs you get on your content, the more you'll show up in the results, and when the paying person is searching for an answer, boom! There you are. So you give people what they want, and it furthers your purpose. If people don't want to spend money, it's ok. They're investing in themselves by consuming your content. They're learning and growing, and you're going to shift them. Being around what you create every day will give them what they need. It'll be slower than if you're working one on one, but they're also putting the time in daily so you'll help them. You'll change their lives even if you never meet them. They'll feel like you're their mentor, friend, and guide even though you'll have no idea who they are. And for those who want access to you, they will pay for it, and you can build a business around it. That money will let you create even more content to help even more people. Your purpose will spread and be felt around the world.

Your purpose is important and making money from it helps you help more people.

MAKING MONEY FROM YOUR PURPOSE

"If a person gets his attitude toward money straight,
it will help straighten out almost every other area
in his life."

—BILLY GRAHAM

Your purpose is too important to just be a hobby.

It fills your soul to help the people who are going through what you've been through. You have a choice to either serve on a part-time basis in the evenings and on the weekends while you hold down a job that isn't fulfilling to you, or you can turn this deep purpose of yours into a business, learn to make money doing it, eventually hire people to join you on your team, and create an organization that helps people around the world.

You start at the start.

You don't need money to start. You invest your resourcefulness, not your resources. You start with a service that gets you close to your customers. You get your first clients using the *Fast Pass to Freedom*, creating partnerships and alliances, and by being a thought leader. You take what's in your head, the *Recipe for Success* that saved you, and you teach it to others while getting paid to do it. Then you expand into more services and products that will change the world.

You deserve this.

By helping others, it makes the pain you went through mean something. It doesn't own you anymore. Your struggles are being turned into triumph. You're taking coal and transforming it to diamonds. I'm so excited to see your journey expand, the people you help blossom, and the impact that you have explode. You deserve this. Now go out and get it!

That's how you turn your purpose into profits. Did you catch all of it? Here are the quick highlights.

SECTION HIGHLIGHTS: TURNING YOUR PURPOSE INTO PROFITS

"For me, money is not my definition of success. Inspiring people is a definition of success."

—KANYE WEST

Turning Your Purpose into Profits Highlights

- If you never learn how to make money, you'll always end up having to have a job to make money and end up doing your purpose only as a hobby.
- You invest your heart, your hustle, your energy, your passion—but not your money. Don't spend your money until you're making money.
- Entrepreneurship is always about resourcefulness more than resources.
- Break the problem you're facing down into the smallest next step.
- A great way to start with no money is with a service, not a product.
- Starting a service also gets you close to your customer.

- The most important element in your content is the information. Does the content make me feel? Does it make me think? Does it resonate? Does it make me believe that you can help me?
- Every social media platform has a search function. Who is posting about the topic you're an expert at? What are they struggling with? Can you help? If yes, reach out.
- Super-connectors are people that can recommend you to their audience, so your message goes out to hundreds, thousands, or even millions of people.
- Start by hanging out where they hang out. Ignore all their other accounts and just focus on that one. Their focus becomes your focus.
- "The lens in which we are making that decision is through the lens of our people." (Howard Schultz)
- Being a "thought leader" means you're an expert.
- If you're focused on one platform at a time and you learn how to make great content, you're going to win.
- You need to hit me right away. Immediately. You must lead with your powerful opinion. Make me feel and think something powerful from your very first sentence. You need to capture me with the way you think and pull me in so I want to learn more.
- You will never be 100 percent certain. The only way to know for sure is by looking backwards.
- Good stories build familiarity and trust. I see myself in your story and feel like I'm just like who you were.
- Uncertainty kills action.
- Assume people have questions and answer them inside your content.

- If you started your day with the thing that made you feel bold, powerful, and unstoppable, your life will look dramatically different one year from today.

YOU'RE READY FOR AMAZING THINGS!

"Congratulations! Today is your day. You're off to Great Places! You're off and away! You have brains in your head. You have feet in your shoes. You can steer yourself any direction you choose. You're on your own. And you know what you know. And YOU are the [one] who'll decide where to go."

—DR. SEUSS

Wow, what a journey!

We've gone through a lot together in this book, and I hope you're as excited for your future as I am. I think you're a genius. I think you have Michael Jordan-level talent. I think you have a powerful mission and message that the world needs to hear.

It's time to find it. It's time to embrace it. It's time to stop living someone else's version of your life. It's time to stop playing small. It's time to stop being afraid. You've got this. I #Believe in you.

You know your *Who*. You're deeply rooted in your core value that nobody is going to move you from. You're going to

259

stop caring what people think of you and start living life on your own terms.

You know your *Why*. That pain you went through was actually the best thing for you. It set you on this path to where you are right now, and you're perfectly positioned to take that pain and make sure that so many people don't suffer anymore.

You know your *How*. Everything you struggled with, everything you tried, everything you experimented with is now something you can teach other people. You have your *Recipe for Success* that will make the lives of others so much easier.

And you know how to turn your purpose into profits. You deserve to make money from this. That money will help you live the life you want, build a company, hire a team, and impact the lives of so many more people than if you're just volunteering your time in the evenings and weekends.

"Congratulations! Today is your day. You're off to Great Places! You're off and away!"

THE END

"Now this is not the end. It is not even the beginning of the end. But it is, perhaps, the end of the beginning."

—WINSTON CHURCHILL

Congratulations on reaching the end! Here are a few ideas for you to consider:

1. If you haven't emailed your receipt or a picture of you with the book yet, send it to **serve@evancarmichael.com** to get your *free bonuses*.

2. I'd love to have your help spreading the message. If you read the book, **please consider sharing it** with your friends and online so that more people can learn the wisdom here that is essential but not taught in schools. If you create any videos or posts, tag me in them. I'd love to see what you thought of the book and how it's helping you!

3. If you got great value from this book consider buying a copy for a friend. Some people are making this book a part of their customer service, where all new customers get a copy of the book as a thank you. If it made a meaningful difference for you, it'll make a meaningful

difference for others and **you'll be remembered** as the person who introduced them to it.

4. Most important of all, **take action**. Don't let this book just sit on your shelf collecting dust. Do something. You don't get changes in your life or business by just reading. You get the changes you want by taking action.

I can't wait to see and hear about your progress. You're going to change the world, and I'm honored to play a tiny part in your journey.

Much love,
Evan.
#Believe

ABOUT EVAN CARMICHAEL

"Evan consumes so much content and then knows
how to DJ it to inspire people."

—GARY VAYNERCHUK

Evan Carmichael #Believes in entrepreneurs...

At nineteen, he built then sold a biotech software company. At
twenty-two, he was a venture capitalist raising $500,000 to $15
million. He is the author of *Your One Word*, runs a YouTube
channel with over two million subscribers, and speaks glob-
ally. He wants to solve the world's biggest problem: people don't
#Believe in themselves enough. He's set two world records, uses
a trampoline and stand-up desk, owns Canada's largest salsa-
dancing studio, and has a giant Doritos bag in front of him all day
long to remind him that he's stronger than the Doritos. Toronto
is his home. He's a husband, father, TSM Fan, and a League of
Legends Teemo main.